READING
COMPREHENSION
WORKSHOP
REFLECTIONS

GLOBE FEARON
EDUCATIONAL PUBLISHER
PARAMUS, NEW JERSEY

Paramount

Paramount Publishing

Executive Editor: Virginia Seeley
Senior Editor: Bernice Golden
Editor: Lynn W. Kloss
Editorial Assistant: Roger Weisman
Product Development: Book Production Systems
Art Director: Nancy Sharkey
Production Manager: Penny Gibson
Production Editors: Nicole Cypher, Eric Dawson
Marketing Manager: Sandra Hutchison
Photo Research: Jenifer Hixson
Electronic Page Production: Siren Design
Cover Design: Carol Anson
Cover Illustration: Jennifer Bolten

Globe Fearon Educational Publisher wishes to thank the following copyright owners for permission to reproduce copyrighted selections in this book: **Black Sparrow Press**, for Wanda Coleman, "Poetry Lesson Number One" from *Heavy Daughter Blues: Poems and Stories 1968-1986*, copyright (c) 1987 by Wanda Coleman; **The Chicago Defender**, for Dean Babs Fafunwa, "An African's Adventures in America," reprinted in *Young and Black in America* (Random House), (c) 1967 The Chicago Defender, (c) 1971 Random House, Inc.; **Leo Dangel**, for Leo Dangel, "Gaining Yardage," from *Preposterous Poems of Youth*, selected by Paul Janeczko, originally published in *Old Man Brunner Country* (Spoon River Poetry Press), copyright (c) 1987 by Leo Dangel; **Harcourt Brace and Company** for Gary Soto, "The No-Guitar Blues" from *Baseball in April and Other Stories*, copyright (c) 1990 by Gary Soto; **Harold Ober Associates Inc.**, for Langston Hughes, "Thank You, M'am," from *The Langston Hughes Reader*, copyright (c) 1958 Langston Hughes, copyright renewed 1986 by George Houston Bass; **The Reader's Digest Association, Inc.**, for Armando Socarra Ramírez, "Stowaway," from *The Reader's Digest*, January 1970, (c) The Reader's Digest Association, Inc., 1969; **Walker and Company, 435 Hudson Street, New York, NY 10014, (800) 289-2553**, for Isaac Asimov, "Sarah Tops," from *The Keyword and Other Mysteries*, copyright (c) 1977 by Isaac Asimov.

Globe Fearon Educational Publisher wishes to thank the following copyright owners for permission to reproduce illustrations and photographs in this book: **p. 16**: Illustration by David Tamura; **p. 49**: Photograph by Art Resource; **p. 50**: Photograph by Werner Forman / Art Resource; **p. 64**: Photograph, (c) MAAK Studios, M.R. Baham, Southern Stock Photo Agency; **p. 67**: Map by Mapping Specialists; **p. 82**: Photograph, courtesy Lindamichellebaron; **p. 99**: Photograph, © Richard Vogel / Gamma Liaison; **p. 114**: Illustration by Kenneth Spengler.

Printed in the United States of America   3 4 5 6 7 8 9 10 99 98 97

ISBN: 0-835-90564-0

GLOBE FEARON
EDUCATIONAL PUBLISHER
PARAMUS, NEW JERSEY

Paramount Publishing

Contents

Unit ONE

BECOMING AN ACTIVE READER

Good readers are active readers. They become involved when they read a **short story** by creating pictures in their minds of the story's characters and settings. They often feel as if they can join in story conversations.

Using Skills and Strategies

Asking questions about **story conflict** can help you understand a story's plot. You may ask: What problem does the main character face? How does the character try to resolve, or deal with, this problem? How is it resolved?

Writers use **idioms**, or expressions that mean something different from the dictionary definitions of their words, to make writing sound like speech. You may ask: Why did the author use idioms in this story? How do other words in the story help me understand the idioms? How do idioms add color to the writing?

In this unit, identifying **story conflict** and interpreting **idioms** will help you read the stories actively.

The Short Story: The Writer's Voice

Short stories can help readers learn about other cultures. They learn how other people think, act, and feel. You will find that the problems and values of other cultures have much in common with your own. Recognizing these similarities can help you understand other people's ideas and experiences better.

Responding to Short Stories

Good readers often find themselves laughing out loud, getting nervous, or even crying as they read. Jot down your thoughts and feelings in the side margins as you read "The No-Guitar Blues" and "Thank You, M'am." Writing sidenotes will help you remember your reactions to the stories. Refer to these notes as you discuss the stories with your classmates.

Story Conflict

Introducing Strategies

The main character in a story usually faces a problem, or **conflict**. The actions that the character takes to **resolve**, or deal with, this conflict often determine the story's plot. Understanding conflict helps you learn about the story, about human nature, and about yourself. As you read, ask yourself questions like these: What problem does the character have? How is this conflict resolved?

You can use a diagram like the one below to map the main character's conflicts in a story.

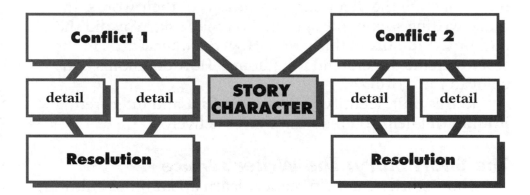

Reading the Story

Read "The No-Guitar Blues" and the sidenotes on pages 8-13. The sidenotes show what one reader thought about conflict in the story. Use these sidenotes to answer the questions below.

1. What details from the story does the reader use to guess what the story's conflict might be?

_____

_____

2. How does understanding Fausto's conflict help the reader understand the story?

_____

_____

Practicing Story Conflict

A. The quotations below are about Fausto's conflicts in "The No-Guitar Blues." Read each quotation and circle the letter of the true statement. On the line below each item, explain your answer.

1. "He couldn't ask his parents because they would just say, 'Money doesn't grow on trees' or 'What do you think we are, bankers?' And besides, they hated rock music."

    a. Fausto's conflict, or problem, is that he does not like his parents.

    b. Fausto's conflict, or problem, is that his parents don't see the situation as he does.

_____

2. "Fausto looked at the bill and knew he was in trouble. Not with these nice folks or with his parents but with himself."

    a. The conflict over the money takes place in Fausto's mind.

    b. The conflict over the money takes place between Fausto and the owners of the dog.

_____

3. "He ironed it between his palms, and dropped it into the basket. The grown-ups stared."

    a. Fausto hopes to resolve his conflict by giving the money to the church.

    b. The grown-ups stare because they know that Fausto has been dishonest.

_____

B. On the lines below, write about a movie or TV show in which one of the characters had to make a decision between right and wrong. Describe the conflict and how the character resolved it.

_____

_____

_____

_____

_____

_____

Applying *Story Conflict*

A. Read the following passage. Then answer the questions that follow it.

Dorrie wanted to tell Mrs. Darnay why she couldn't make play practice tonight. It was the dress rehearsal, the most important practice of all. This was the night Dorrie had been waiting for. Her dreams of having the lead in the show had come true. How she had wanted to be in the play! Now it was over. All over.

She couldn't face Mrs. Darnay. The words just wouldn't come. How could she tell her favorite teacher that her brother was in jail? That she would have to watch Carlee and Roger while her mom went to meet with the legal assistance people? Dorrie slammed her locker shut and walked quickly past the auditorium door. . . .

1. Identify two conflicts that Dorrie faces.

_____

_____

2. What story details helped you identify these conflicts?

_____

_____

B. Write a paragraph to tell how you think Dorrie can resolve her conflicts. Give reasons to support your ideas.

_____

_____

_____

_____

_____

_____

_____

_____

_____

To review

↓

page 18

Idioms

Introducing Strategies

*Denny **jumped out of his skin** when I slipped up behind him in the spooky cave and tapped him on the shoulder.*

In the sentence above, the words in bold type mean something different from their literal, or dictionary, meaning. Writers often use these phrases, called **idioms**, to make their writing sound like informal speech. You can use context—words and ideas near the idioms—to figure out the meaning of idioms. The chart below can help you use context clues to figure out the meanings of idioms and to check your guesses.

Question	Look Back	Meaning	Confirm
What words don't mean exactly what they say?	What words might show what the idiom means?	What does the idiom mean?	Does the idiom make sense in the story?

Reading the Story

Reread "The No-Guitar Blues" on pages 8-13. As you read, underline idioms, or phrases that do not mean exactly what they say. Then answer the questions below.

1. Identify one idiom you found while reading "The No-Guitar Blues" and tell what it means.

_____

_____

_____

2. What context clues did you use to help you figure out the idiom's meaning?

_____

_____

_____

Practicing Idioms

A. In each pair of sentences below, one contains an idiom and the other does not. Circle the letter of the sentence that contains the idiom and underline the idiom. Then explain the idiom's meaning on the lines that follow.

1. a. They would tell Fausto that they had no money.
   b. They would tell Fausto that money doesn't grow on trees.

   _____

   _____

2. a. The dog blinked a pair of sad eyes and whined.
   b. "What's the matter? Cat got your tongue?"

   _____

   _____

3. a. At that moment a dim light came on inside Fausto's head.
   b. He realized it was winter and no one would hire him.

   _____

   _____

4. a. He would say he had found Roger near the freeway.
   b. That would scare the daylights out of the owners, who would be so happy that they would probably give him a reward.

   _____

   _____

B. On the lines below, write another sentence from the story that contains an idiom. Next, rewrite the sentence so that it expresses the same meaning without the idiom.

   _____

   _____

   _____

   _____

   _____

   _____

Applying Idioms

A. Read the paragraph below and underline each idiom you find. Then, on the lines that follow, list four idioms and write their meanings.

> As usual, Wayne had bitten off more than he could chew. He shouldn't have told everyone he would make all the posters for the car wash. The Computer Club needed to publicize the event. The club's annual car wash was always a big hit. The money would be spent on new software. But he was really in a pickle now. How could he get the posters done in time? He was feeling down in the dumps as he slowly walked home.

1. _____

_____

_____

2. _____

_____

_____

3. _____

_____

_____

4. _____

_____

_____

B. Think of an idiom you might use in everyday speech. Write the idiom and tell what it means.

_____

_____

_____

_____

_____

_____

_____

To review

↓

page 20

Gary Soto (1952-   ) was born in the San Joaquin Valley in California. Soto is Mexican-American, or Chicano, and much of his writing is about his people. This story is taken from *Baseball in April and Other Stories*, a collection of short stories for young people.

The No-Guitar Blues

by Gary Soto

The notes in the margins show how one reader identified the conflicts Fausto faces.

The moment Fausto saw the group Los Lobos on "American Bandstand," he knew exactly what he wanted to do with his life—play guitar. His eyes grew large with excitement as Los Lobos ground out a song while teenagers bounced off each other on the crowded dance floor.

He had watched "American Bandstand" for years and had heard Ray Camacho and the Teardrops at Romain Playground, but it had never occurred to him that he too might become a musician. That afternoon Fausto knew his mission in life: to play guitar in his own band; to sweat out his songs and prance around the stage; to make money and dress weird.

Fausto turned off the television set and walked outside, wondering how he could get enough money to buy a guitar. He couldn't ask his parents because they would just say, "Money doesn't grow on trees" or "What

▶ do you think we are, bankers?" And besides, they hated rock music. They were into the *conjunto* music of Lydia Mendoza, Flaco Jimenez, and Little Joe and La Familia. And, as Fausto recalled, the last album they bought was *The Chipmunks Sing Christmas Favorites*.

Fausto wants a guitar but doesn't have the money to buy one. This may be a conflict in the story.

But what the heck, he'd give it a try. He returned inside and watched his mother make tortillas. He leaned against the kitchen counter, trying to work up the nerve to ask her for a guitar. Finally, he couldn't hold back any longer.

"Mom," he said, "I want a guitar for Christmas."

She looked up from rolling tortillas. "Honey, a guitar

It looks as if Fausto's parents will ▶ costs a lot of money."
tell him he will have to find the money himself. I wonder what he will do to earn it.

"How 'bout for my birthday next year," he tried again.

"I can't promise," she said, turning back to her tortillas, "but we'll see."

It seems like earning money ▶ Fausto walked back outside with a buttered tortilla. He
won't be easy for Fausto. I think knew his mother was right. His father was a warehouseman
I was right about this being a at Berven Rugs, where he made good money but not
source of conflict.

enough to buy everything his children wanted. Fausto decided to mow lawns to earn money, and was pushing the mower down the street before he realized it was winter and no one would hire him. He returned the mower and picked up a rake. He hopped onto his sister's bike (his had two flat tires) and rode north to the nicer section of Fresno in search of work. He went door-to-door, but after three hours he managed to get only one job, and not to rake leaves. He was asked to hurry down to the store to buy a loaf of bread, for which he received a grimy, dirt-caked quarter.

He also got an orange, which he ate sitting at the curb. While he was eating, a dog walked up and sniffed his leg. Fausto pushed him away and threw an orange peel skyward. The dog caught it and ate it in one gulp. The dog looked at Fausto and wagged his tail for more. Fausto tossed him a slice of orange, and the dog snapped it up and licked his lips.

"How come you like oranges, dog?"

The dog blinked a pair of sad eyes and whined.

"What's the matter? Cat got your tongue?" Fausto laughed at his joke and offered the dog another slice.

At that moment a dim light came on inside Fausto's head. He saw that it was sort of a fancy dog, a terrier or something, with dog tags and a shiny collar. And it looked well fed and healthy. In his neighborhood, the dogs were never licensed, and if they got sick they were placed near the water heater until they got well.

This dog looked like he belonged to rich people. Fausto cleaned his juice-sticky hands on his pants and got to his feet. The light in his head grew brighter. It just might work. He called the dog, patted its muscular back, and bent down to check the license.

"Great," he said. "There's an address."

The dog's name was Roger, which struck Fausto as weird because he'd never heard of a dog with a human name. Dogs should have names like Bomber, Freckles, Queenie, Killer, and Zero.

Fausto planned to take the dog home and collect a reward. He would say he had found Roger near the freeway. That would scare the daylights out of the owners, who would be so happy that they would probably give him a reward. He felt bad about lying, but the dog *was* loose. And it might even really be lost, because the address was six blocks away.

Fausto stashed the rake and his sister's bike behind a bush, and, tossing an orange peel every time Roger

◄ Fausto has an idea. I think it may have something to do with the dog belonging to rich people. It sounds like the idea may not be honest.

◄ Yes, his idea isn't honest. He's going to pretend the dog is lost and collect a reward.

Write your own sidenotes as you read the rest of the story. In your notes, comment on the conflicts Fausto faces and the ways he resolves them.

became distracted, walked the dog to his house. He hesitated on the porch until Roger began to scratch the door with a muddy paw. Fausto had come this far, so he figured he might as well go through with it. He knocked softly. When no one answered, he rang the doorbell. A man in a silky bathrobe and slippers opened the door and seemed confused by the sight of his dog and the boy.

"Sir," Fausto said, gripping Roger by the collar. "I found your dog by the freeway. His dog license says he lives here." Fausto looked down at the dog, then up to the man. "He does, doesn't he?"

The man stared at Fausto a long time before saying in a pleasant voice, "That's right." He pulled his robe tighter around him because of the cold and asked Fausto to come in. "So he was by the freeway?"

"Uh-huh."

"You bad, snoopy dog," said the man, wagging his finger. "You probably knocked over some trash cans, too, didn't you?"

Fausto didn't say anything. He looked around, amazed by this house with its shiny furniture and a television as large as the front window at home. Warm bread smells filled the air and music full of soft tinkling floated in from another room.

"Helen," the man called to the kitchen. "We have a visitor." His wife came into the living room wiping her hands on a dish towel and smiling. "And who have we here?" she asked in one of the softest voices Fausto had ever heard.

"This young man said he found Roger near the freeway."

Fausto repeated his story to her while staring at a perpetual clock with a bell-shaped glass, the kind his aunt got when she celebrated her twenty-fifth anniversary. The lady frowned and said, wagging a finger at Roger, "Oh, you're a bad boy."

"It was very nice of you to bring Roger home," the man said. "Where do you live?"

"By that vacant lot on Olive," he said. "You know, by Brownie's Flower Place."

The wife looked at her husband, then Fausto. Her eyes twinkled triangles of light as she said, "Well, young man, you're probably hungry. How about a turnover?"

"What do I have to turn over?" Fausto asked, thinking she was talking about yard work or something like turning over trays of dried raisins.

"No, no, dear, it's a pastry." She took him by the elbow and guided him to a kitchen that sparkled with copper pans and bright yellow wallpaper. She guided him to the kitchen table and gave him a tall glass of milk and something that looked like an *empanada*. Steamy waves of heat escaped when he tore it in two. He ate with both eyes on the man and woman who stood arm in arm smiling at him. They were strange, he thought. But nice.

"That was good," he said after he finished the turnover. "Did you make it, ma'am?"

"Yes, I did. Would you like another?"

"No, thank you. I have to go home now."

As Fausto walked to the door, the man opened his wallet and took out a bill. "This is for you," he said. "Roger is very special to us, almost like a son."

Fausto looked at the bill and knew he was in trouble. Not with these nice folks or with his parents but with himself. How could he have been so deceitful? The dog wasn't lost. It was just having a fun Saturday walking around.

"I can't take that."

"You have to. You deserve it, believe me," the man said.

"No, I don't."

"Now don't be silly," said the lady. She took the bill from her husband and stuffed it into Fausto's shirt pocket. "You're a lovely child. Your parents are lucky to have you. Be good. And come see us again, please."

Fausto went out, and the lady closed the door. Fausto clutched the bill through his shirt pocket. He felt like ringing the doorbell and begging them to please take the money back, but he knew they would refuse. He hurried away, and at the end of the block, pulled the bill from his shirt pocket: it was a crisp twenty-dollar bill.

"Oh, man, I shouldn't have lied," he said under his breath as he started up the street like a zombie. He wanted to run to church for Saturday confession, but it was past four-thirty, when confession stopped.

He returned to the bush where he had hidden the rake and his sister's bike and rode home slowly, not daring to touch the money in his pocket. At home, in the privacy of his room, he examined the twenty-dollar bill. He had never had so much money. It was probably enough to buy a secondhand guitar. But he felt bad, like the time he stole a dollar from the secret fold inside his older brother's wallet.

Fausto went outside and sat on the fence. "Yeah," he said. "I can probably get a guitar for twenty. Maybe at a yard sale—things are cheaper."

His mother called him to dinner.

The next day he dressed for church without anyone telling him. He was going to go to eight o'clock mass.

"I'm going to church, Mom," he said. His mother was in the kitchen cooking *papas* and *chorizo con huevos*. A pile of tortillas lay warm under a dish-towel.

"Oh, I'm so proud of you, my son." She beamed, turning over the crackling *papas*.

His older brother, Lawrence, who was at the table reading the funnies, mimicked, "Oh, I'm so proud of you, my son," under his breath.

At Saint Theresa's he sat near the front. When Father Jerry began by saying that we are all sinners, Fausto thought he looked straight at him. Could he know? Fausto fidgeted with guilt. No, he thought. I only did it yesterday.

Fausto knelt, prayed, and sang. But he couldn't forget the man and the lady, whose names he didn't even know, and the *empanada* they had given him. It had a strange name but tasted really good. He wondered how they got rich. And how that dome clock worked. He had asked his mother once how his aunt's clock worked. She said it just worked, the way the refrigerator works. It just did.

Fausto caught his mind wandering and tried to concentrate on his sins. He said a Hail Mary and sang, and when the wicker basket came his way, he stuck a hand reluctantly in his pocket and pulled out the twenty-dollar bill. He ironed it between his palms, and dropped it into the basket. The grown-ups stared. Here was a kid dropping twenty dollars in the basket while they gave just three or four dollars.

There would be a second collection for Saint Vincent de Paul, the lector announced. The wicker baskets again floated in the pews, and this time the adults around him, given a second chance to show their charity, dug deep into their wallets and purses and dropped in fives and tens. This time Fausto tossed in the grimy quarter.

Fausto felt better after church. He went home and played football in the front yard with his brother and some neighbor kids. He felt cleared of wrongdoing and was so happy that he played one of his best games of football ever. On one play, he tore his good pants, which he knew he shouldn't have been wearing. For a second, while he examined the hole, he wished he hadn't given the twenty dollars away.

Man, I coulda bought me some Levi's, he thought. He pictured his twenty dollars being spent to buy church candles. He pictured a priest buying an armful of flowers with *his* money.

Fausto had to forget about getting a guitar. He spent the next day playing soccer in his good pants, which were now his old pants. But that night during dinner, his mother said she remembered seeing an old bass guitarron the last time she cleaned out her father's garage.

"It's a little dusty," his mom said, serving his favorite enchiladas, "But I think it works. Grandpa says it works."

Fausto's ears perked up. That was the same kind the guy in Los Lobos played. Instead of asking for the guitar, he waited for his mother to offer it to him. And she did, while gathering the dishes from the table.

"No, Mom, I'll do it," he said, hugging her. "I'll do the dishes forever if you want."

It was the happiest day of his life. No, it was the second-happiest day of his life. The happiest was when his grandfather Lupe placed the guitarron, which was nearly as huge as a washtub, in his arms. Fausto ran a thumb down the strings, which vibrated in his throat and chest. It sounded beautiful, deep and eerie. A pumpkin smile widened on his face.

"OK, *hijo*, now you put your fingers like this," said his grandfather, smelling of tobacco and after-shave. He took Fausto's fingers and placed them on the strings. Fausto strummed a chord on the guitarron, and the bass resounded in their chests.

The guitarron was more complicated than Fausto imagined. But he was confident that after a few more lessons he could start a band that would someday play on "American Bandstand" for the dancing crowds.

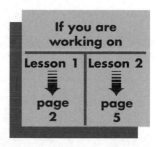

If you are
working on

Lesson 1 | Lesson 2

page 2 | page 5

Thank You, M'am

by Langston Hughes

Use the margins to write your own notes about the conflicts the characters face and how they resolve these conflicts.

She was a large woman with a large purse that had everything in it but hammer and nails. It had a long strap and she carried it slung across her shoulder. It was about eleven o'clock at night, and she was walking alone, when a boy ran up behind her and tried to snatch her purse. The strap broke with the single tug the boy gave it from behind. But the boy's weight, and the weight of the purse combined caused him to lose his balance so, instead of taking off full blast as he had hoped, the boy fell on his back on the sidewalk, and his legs flew up. The large woman simply turned around and kicked him right square in his blue jeaned sitter. Then she reached down, picked the boy up by his shirt front, and shook him until his teeth rattled.

After that the woman said, "Pick up my pocketbook, boy, and give it here."

She still held him. But she bent down enough to permit him to stoop and pick up her purse. Then she said, "Now ain't you ashamed of yourself?"

Firmly gripped by his shirt front, the boy said, "Yes'm."

The woman said, "What did you want to do it for?"

The boy said, "I didn't aim to."

She said, "You a lie!"

By that time two or three people passed, stopped, turned to look, and some stood watching.

"If I turn you loose, will you run?" asked the woman.

"Yes'm," said the boy.

"Then I won't turn you loose," said the woman. She did not release him.

"I'm very sorry, lady, I'm sorry," whispered the boy.

"Um-hum! And your face is dirty. I got a great mind to wash your face for you. Ain't you got nobody home to tell you to wash your face?"

"No'm," said the boy.

"Then it will get washed this evening," said the large woman starting up the street, dragging the frightened boy behind her.

He looked as if he were fourteen or fifteen, frail and willow-wild, in tennis shoes and blue jeans.

The woman said, "You ought to be my son. I would teach you right from wrong. Least I can do right now is to wash your face. Are you hungry?"

"No'm," said the being-dragged boy. "I just want you to turn me loose."

"Was I bothering *you* when I turned that corner?" asked the woman.

"No'm."

"But you put yourself in contact with *me*," said the woman. "If you think that that contact is not going to last awhile, you got another thought coming. When I get through with you, sir, you are going to remember Mrs. Luella Bates Washington Jones."

Sweat popped out on the boy's face and he began to struggle. Mrs. Jones stopped, jerked him around in front of her, put a half-nelson about his neck, and continued to drag him up the street. When she got to her door, she dragged the boy inside, down a hall, and into a large kitchenette-furnished room at the rear of the house. She switched on the light and left the door open. The boy could hear other roomers laughing and talking in the large house. Some of their doors were open, too, so he knew he and the woman were not alone. The woman still had him by the neck in the middle of her room.

She said, "What is your name?"

"Roger," answered the boy.

"Then, Roger, you go to that sink and wash your face," said the woman, whereupon she turned him loose—at last. Roger looked at the door—looked at the woman—looked at the door—*and went to the sink.*

"Let the water run until it gets warm," she said. "Here's a clean towel."

"You gonna take me to jail?" asked the boy, bending over the sink.

"Not with that face, I would not take you nowhere," said the woman. "Here I am trying to get home to cook me a bite to eat and you snatch my pocketbook! Maybe you ain't been to your supper either, late as it be. Have you?"

"There's nobody home at my house," said the boy.

"Then we'll eat," said the woman. "I believe you're hungry—or been hungry—to try to snatch my pocketbook."

"I wanted a pair of blue suede shoes," said the boy.

"Well, you didn't have to snatch *my* pocketbook to get some suede shoes," said Mrs. Luella Bates Washington Jones. "You could of asked me."

"M'am?"

The water dripping from his face, the boy looked at her. There was a long pause. A very long pause. After he had dried his face and not knowing what else to do dried it again, the boy turned around, wondering what next. The door was open. He could make a dash for it down the hall. He could run, run, run, run, *run!*

The woman was sitting on the day-bed. After awhile she said, "I were young once and I wanted things I could not get."

There was another long pause. The boy's mouth opened. Then he frowned, but not knowing he frowned.

The woman said, "Um-hum! You thought I was going to say *but,* didn't you? You thought I was going to say, *but I didn't snatch people's pocketbooks.* Well, I wasn't going to say that." Pause. Silence. "I have done things, too, which I would not tell you, son—neither tell God, if he didn't already know. So you set down while I fix us something to eat. You might run that comb through your hair so you will look presentable."

In another corner of the room behind a screen was a gas plate and an icebox. Mrs. Jones got up and went behind the screen. The woman did not watch the boy to see if he was going to run now, nor did she watch her purse which she left behind her on the day-bed. But the boy took care to sit on the far side of the room where he thought she could easily see him out of the corner of her eye, if she wanted to. He did not trust the woman *not* to trust him. And he did not want to be mistrusted now.

"Do you need somebody to go to the store," asked the boy, "maybe to get some milk or something?"

"Don't believe I do," said the woman, "unless you just want sweet milk yourself. I was going to make cocoa out of this canned milk I got here."

"That will be fine," said the boy.

She heated some lima beans and ham she had in the icebox, made the cocoa, and set the table. The woman did not ask the boy anything about where he lived, or his folks, or anything else that would embarrass him. Instead, as they ate, she told him about her job in a hotel beauty-shop that stayed open late, what the work was like, and how all kinds of women came in and out, blondes, red-heads, and Spanish. Then she cut him a half of her ten-cent cake.

"Eat some more, son," she said.

When they were finished eating she got up and said, "Now, here, take this ten dollars and buy yourself some blue suede shoes. And next time, do not make the mistake of latching onto *my* pocketbook *nor nobody else's*— because shoes come by devilish like that will burn your feet. I got to get my rest now. But I wish you would behave yourself, son, from here on in."

She led him down the hall to the front door and opened it. "Goodnight! Behave yourself, boy!" she said, looking out into the street.

The boy wanted to say something else other than, "Thank you, m'am," to Mrs. Luella Bates Washington Jones, but he couldn't do so as he turned at the barren stoop and looked back at the large woman in the door. He barely managed to say, "Thank you," before she shut the door. And he never saw her again.

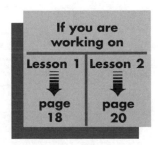

If you are working on

Lesson 1	Lesson 2
⬇	⬇
page 18	page 20

Reviewing Story Conflict

A. Read the story "Thank You, M'am" on pages 14-17. As you read, record your notes about the conflicts Roger faces in the margins. Then use these notes to complete the diagram below.

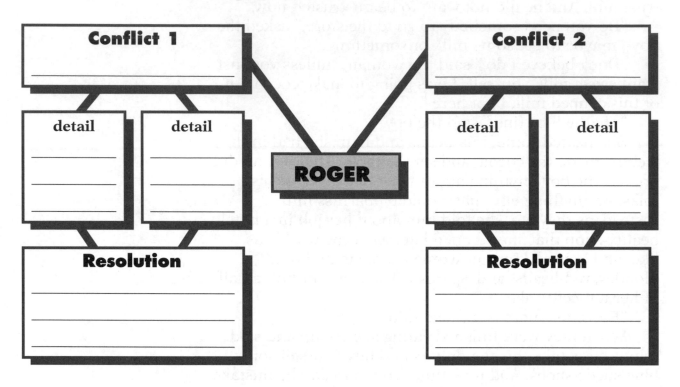

B. Use your diagram to help you explain how Roger resolves his conflicts. Use story details to support your answer.

_____

_____

_____

_____

_____

_____

_____

_____

_____

_____

Testing Story Conflict

A. Read each statement below. Fill in the bubble of each statement you think is true. If you do not think a statement is true, leave the bubble empty. Then explain your answer on the lines that follow each question.

○ **1.** One conflict Roger faces is wanting a pair of blue suede shoes.

_____

_____

_____

○ **2.** Once Mrs. Jones catches Roger, his conflict is whether or not he should lie about why he wanted the money.

_____

_____

_____

○ **3.** Another conflict Roger faces is whether or not to make a dash out of Mrs. Jones's room.

_____

_____

_____

○ **4.** After Mrs. Jones takes Roger home he has a new conflict: He wants her to trust him.

_____

_____

_____

B. Why do you think Roger says "Thank you, m'am" to Mrs. Jones? For what is he thankful? Explain your answer on the lines below.

_____

_____

_____

_____

_____

To begin
Lesson 2
▼
page
5

Reviewing *Idioms*

A. Each passage below contains an idiom. Read the passage, then use the strategy outlined on the chart to figure out the idiom's meaning. Write your responses on the chart.

1. Harry tried to explain why he was in the hall during class, but he just put his foot in his mouth. He had forgotten about the hall pass in his pocket.

2. Juana's mom sat down on the bed and said softly, "I'm sorry I can't let you go. We don't have the money." Juana knew her mom would have said yes if she could. Mom's heart was in the right place.

Question	Look Back	Meaning	Confirm
1. _____	1. _____	1. _____	1. _____
2. _____	2. _____	2. _____	2. _____

B. On the lines below, write a paragraph in which you describe a song you like. When you have finished, reread your writing and circle the idioms you used.

_____

_____

_____

_____

_____

_____

_____

Testing Idioms

A. Find the idiom in each numbered sentence below, and circle the sentence that best restates its meaning. On the lines that follow, explain your choice.

1. Gregory was up to his ears in homework this week.
   a. He had lots of homework.
   b. His homework was about ears and how they function.
   c. Gregory had less homework than usual.
   d. Gregory had so much homework that his ears hurt.

   _____

2. Mrs. Perez bent over backwards to help others.
   a. Mrs. Perez walked with her head bent back.
   b. Mrs. Perez was troubled with a bad back.
   c. Mrs. Perez was extremely considerate and helpful.
   d. Mrs. Perez was a former gymnast.

   _____

3. The pollution problem is a tough nut to crack.
   a. The problem is like a cracked nut.
   b. The problem is hard to solve.
   c. It is a smelly problem.
   d. The problem is full of cracks.

   _____

4. Celeste would have to burn the midnight oil to finish her report on time.
   a. She would have to set her report on fire.
   b. She would have to use more oil on her salad.
   c. She would have to work until midnight.
   d. She would have to stay up late and work hard.

   _____

B. On the lines below, write a humorous incident based on someone's misunderstanding of an idiom. (Hints: "Use your noodle," "as the crow flies," "raining cats and dogs.")

   _____

   _____

   _____

   _____

Unit TWO

BECOMING AN ACTIVE READER

Reading an exciting **short story** is like sitting around a campfire listening to someone tell a tall tale. You try to warn the story's characters of danger or figure out solutions to their problems. Reading short stories can help you recreate that feeling in your own home.

Using Skills and Strategies

Drawing conclusions can help you understand a story. You may ask: What happened? Have I seen a situation like this on TV or read something similar to it? What did it mean then? Has something like this happened to me?

Authors draw you into stories by creating a **problem** that their characters must solve. To understand this problem, you may ask: Who are the characters? What is happening? What can the character do to find a **solution** to the problem?

In this unit, **drawing conclusions** and identifying **problems and solutions** will help you read stories actively.

Reading the Short Story

Even though the setting of a short story may seem different from any place you know, you will find that people all over the world face problems that are similar to your own. You may also find that characters that you think are similar to you react to problems in ways that are unlike any you know. The importance of these stories is that they bring you a better understanding of the world.

Responding to Short Stories

Good readers usually find themselves trying to solve the mystery in a story. Like Sherlock Holmes, they try to follow the clues to a solution. Or like Dr. Watson, they may be amazed by someone else's reasoning. Jot down notes in the side margins about solving the mysteries as you read "Sarah Tops" and "Gabriela's Game." These sidenotes will help you discuss the stories with your classmates.

Drawing Conclusions

Lesson 3	Introducing page 23	Practicing page 24	Applying page 25	Reviewing page 35	Testing page 36

Introducing Strategies

Good readers **draw conclusions** as they read. They combine two types of evidence—details from the story and what they already know—to draw these conclusions. For example, they might read that marsupials are mammals with pockets for carrying their young. They know that kangaroos have pockets. They can conclude that kangaroos are marsupials.

The chart below shows how readers use details from the story and what they already know to draw conclusions.

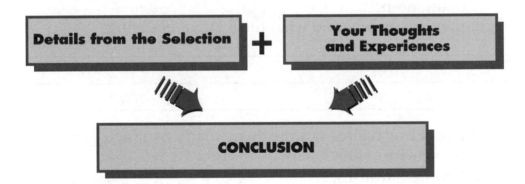

Reading the Story

Read "Sarah Tops" and the sidenotes on pages 29-30. The sidenotes show how one good reader combined details from the story with what he or she already knew to draw conclusions. Use these notes to complete the items below.

1. What clues in the story led the reader to conclude that the police were trying to recover stolen property?

_____

_____

2. What does the reader already know that helped him or her conclude that Sarah will be hard to find?

_____

_____

_____

Practicing Drawing Conclusions

A. Read the excerpt from the story. Then circle the letter next to the word or phrase that best completes each sentence. On the lines below, explain how you used story details and what you already know to draw your conclusion.

> *"The woman who reported the killing . . . said he said three words to her, very slowly, 'Try . . . Sarah . . . Tops.'"*

1. The police look up the names *Tops* and *Topps* in the telephone book because

    a. they know Sarah Tops was involved in the robbery.

    b. Sarah Tops knows who killed the man.

    c. the woman tells them that Sarah Tops knows where the diamond is.

    d. they misunderstand what the woman is saying.

_____

_____

_____

2. The narrator figures out the dying man's message by

    a. breaking its code.

    b. finding Sarah Tops.

    c. finding a word that sounds like "Sarah Tops."

    d. questioning the museum guard.

_____

_____

_____

B. In "Sarah Tops," the woman misunderstands the dying man's words. Write an example of the same type of misunderstanding that you or someone you know has had. For instance, *I scream* might also be heard as *ice cream*.

_____

_____

_____

_____

_____

Applying Drawing Conclusions

A. Read the paragraphs below and answer the questions that follow.

Chiyoko could scarcely believe her eyes. Every item had been taken out of her locker and placed on the floor. She'd had the locker stuffed so full of junk that Mr. Mack, the teacher in charge of halls, had been after her for a month to clean it out. He'd even used words like detention and suspension from the cheerleading squad. But would he have done this?

Nothing seemed to be missing—which was a relief—and no damage done to . . . but wait a minute . . . where were her pompons? Chiyoko had shoved the burgundy and gold shakers in on top of everything after practice last evening. Now, lying on the floor at her feet, were red and black pompons.

1. Give details from the paragraphs to describe what has happened to Chiyoko's locker.

_____

_____

_____

2. What do you think happened to Chiyoko's pompons? How did what you already know help you draw this conclusion?

_____

_____

_____

B. On the lines below, write a conclusion for this story.

_____

_____

_____

_____

_____

_____

_____

_____

To review

↓

page 35

Problem and Solution

Lesson 4	Introducing page 26	Practicing page 27	Applying page 28	Reviewing page 37	Testing page 38

Introducing Strategies

A character in a story usually has a **problem**, or conflict, that needs to be solved. Good readers look at all the parts of a story to try to figure out possible **solutions** to that problem. Before they begin reading, good readers look at the title for clues. As they read, they note important characters and details about the setting, or where the action takes place. Then they try to understand the story's problem. As they continue reading, good readers look for the events that show how the problem is solved.

A story map, such as the one below, can help you see how the characters in a story solve their problems.

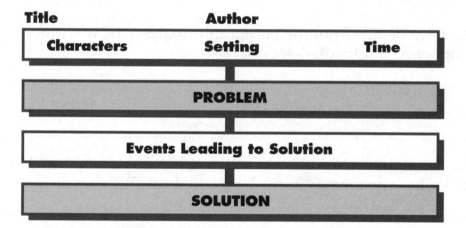

Title   Author

Characters   Setting   Time

PROBLEM

Events Leading to Solution

SOLUTION

Reading the Story

Reread "Sarah Tops" on pages 29-30. As you read, circle information that helps you understand the characters' problems and how they solve them. Use this information to complete the items below.

1. State in your own words the problem that must be solved.

_____

_____

2. Which events lead to the solution of the problem?

_____

_____

Practicing Problem and Solution

A. Fill in the bubble next to each true statement about "Sarah Tops." On the lines that follow, explain your answer.

○ **1.** The title of the story has nothing to do with the solution to the problem.

_____

_____

_____

○ **2.** One important character in the story is already dead when the story begins.

_____

_____

_____

○ **3.** The setting of "Sarah Tops" is not important; the action could take place anywhere.

_____

_____

_____

○ **4.** The solution to the problem in the story involves a dinosaur.

_____

_____

_____

B. How would the problem and solution in this story be different if it were set in a park or a shopping center? What title would you give the rewritten story?

_____

_____

_____

_____

_____

_____

Applying Problem and Solution

A. Read the passage below, which is from a mystery story. Then complete the items that follow it.

Furface sat on top of the tallest bookcase, staring down as the two intruders slipped through the open window. As the smaller of the two men moved toward the desk that held the computer, the other muttered, "There's the computer. The plans must be in there. Take the disks, too." The cat sat without moving.

Suddenly, without warning, Furface leaped at one of the men. Scratching and clawing, she tore at his face. Then, just as quickly, she disappeared out the cat door and down the alley.

1. In your own words, describe what is happening in this story.

_____

_____

2. What do you think the problem of one of the characters might be?

_____

_____

3. Using your answer to #2, write a solution to the character's problem.

_____

_____

B. What clues would you add to this story to help readers solve the problem?

_____

_____

_____

_____

_____

_____

_____

_____

To review
↓
page
37

Few people blended the talents of scientist and writer with greater skill than did Isaac Asimov, who published more than 170 books. The story excerpted below begins when the son of a detective hears about a crime at the Museum of Natural History in New York City. Read to see how the boy's knowledge of science helps solve the case.

Sarah Tops

by Isaac Asimov

. . . Mom looked worried. "There might have been shooting in the museum."

"Well, there wasn't," said Dad soothingly. "This man tried to lose himself in the museum and he didn't succeed."

"I would have," I said, "I know the museum, every inch."

Dad doesn't like me boasting, so he frowned at me. "The thugs who were after him didn't let him get away entirely. They caught up with him outside, knifed him, and got away. We'll catch them, though. We know who they are."

He nodded his head. "They're what's left of the gang that broke into that jewelry store two weeks ago. We managed to get the jewels back, but we didn't grab all the men. And not all the jewels either. One diamond was left. A big one—worth thirty thousand dollars. . . ."

"Did they get the diamond?" I asked.

"How can we tell? The woman who reported the killing came on him when he was just barely able to breathe. She said he said three words to her, very slowly, 'Try . . . Sarah . . . Tops.' Then he died. . . ."

"Is there a Sarah Tops in the phone book, Dad?" I asked.

Dad said, "Did you think we didn't look? No Sarah Tops, either one P or two P's. . . ."

Mom said, "Maybe it's not a person. Maybe it's a firm. Sarah Tops Cakes or something."

"Could be," said Dad. "There's no Sarah Tops firm, but there are other kinds of Tops and they'll be checked out for anyone working there named Sarah. . . ."

And then it hit me. What if. . . .

Dad was just getting up, as if he were going to turn on television, and I said, "Dad, can you get into the museum this time of evening?"

"On police business? Sure."

The notes in the margin show how one good reader used story details and what he or she already knew to draw conclusions about the story.

◀ One of the characters is telling the story, using the word *I*. Based on what they are saying, I think the main character is the detective's son.

◀ They seem to be trying to recover stolen property. This has been the case in other mysteries I've read and seen on TV. It looks like the boy will try to solve the crime.

◀ Here's an important clue. But the man is dead so he can't help. I think the police will have to try to find this Sarah, and I know New York is a huge city. I'm sure it won't be easy.

◀ This has happened in other mysteries I've read. I bet he knows the solution to the mystery and now will show us—like Sherlock Holmes does.

Make notes in the margins about how you combine story details and what you already know to draw conclusions about "Sarah Tops."

"Dad," I said, kind of breathless, "I think we better go look. *Now*. Before the people start coming in again."

"Why?"

"I've got a silly idea. I . . . I . . ."

Dad didn't push me. He likes me to have my own ideas. He thinks maybe I'll be a detective, too, some day. He said, "All right. Let's follow up your lead whatever it is. . . ."

I'd never been in the museum when it was dark. It looked like a huge, underground cave, with the guard's flashlight seeming to make things even darker and more mysterious.

We took the elevator up to the fourth floor where the big shapes loomed in the bit of light that shone this way and that as the guard moved his flash.

"Do you want me to put on the light in this room?" he asked.

"Yes, please," I said.

There they all were. Some in glass cases; but the big ones in the middle of the large room. Bones and teeth and spines of giants that ruled the earth hundreds of millions of years ago.

"I want to look close at that one," I said. "Is it all right if I climb over the railing?"

"Go ahead," said the guard. He helped me.

I leaned against the platform, looking at the grayish plaster material the skeleton was standing on.

"What's this?" I said. It didn't look much different in color from the plaster on which it was lying.

"Chewing gum," said the guard, frowning. "Those darn kids . . ."

"The guy was trying to get away and he saw his chance to throw this . . . keep it away from *them*. . . ." Before I could finish my sentence Dad took the gum from me. He squeezed it, then pulled it apart. Something inside caught the light and flashed. Dad put it in an envelope. "How did you know?" he asked me.

"Well, look at it," I said.

It was a magnificent skeleton. It had a large skull with a bone stretching back over the neck vertebrae. It had two horns over the eyes, and a third one, just a bump, on the snout.

The nameplate said *Triceratops*.

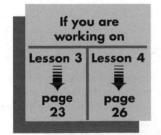

If you are working on

Lesson 3	Lesson 4
⬇	⬇
page 23	page 26

Guadalupe J. Solis is a third-generation Mexican American. A professional writer, Solis also teaches writing at the University of Wisconsin in Milwaukee. He wrote this story for his 12-year-old nephew, Gabriel, who is a fan of mysteries.

Gabriela's Game

by Guadalupe J. Solis, Jr.

As you read, note how story details and your own experiences help you draw conclusions about this story.

Gabriela is my best friend. We have lived next door to each other in the Frink Avenue Apartments all our lives. We're both 14. Our birthdays are only a week apart. Last summer we played a game—Gabriela's game. But let me start at the beginning.

Both of us deliver the evening *Tribune*, and last summer we decided to combine our paper routes into a partnership. Sometimes, while we fold the papers, a story catches Gabriela's eye and she exclaims, "Elena! Here's a Sherlock Holmes crime!" Sherlock Holmes crimes, to Gabriela, are ones that can be investigated just by examining the facts. She likes to try to solve them. I usually humor her and play along. Gabriela wants to be just like her mother, who is a detective for the police force. So Gabriela likes to pay attention to the headlines. She is always looking to see if she can fit together the pieces of a crime just as she imagines her mother does at work.

Anyway, on July 10th at 9:00 P.M., there was a huge fire in another part of town. A row of apartment buildings caught fire and burned to the ground. The next day in Gabriela's kitchen as we folded newspapers, Gabriela read the story aloud. "*Mira*, Elena," Gabriela said, "a Holmes crime!"

"What do you mean? It was a fire." I rolled my eyes at her.

"No, look!" she said, as she held the paper out to me.

"I already read it twice," I told her. "Would you mind just folding the papers and not reading them?"

She threw the paper down and said, "*Estás muy estúpida!* That's why I'm Sherlock Holmes and you're Watson. The paper says that the apartment buildings had been standing there half built for several months. I wonder why someone would start a huge project like that and not finish it."

"Maybe the person ran out of money," I suggested.

"Maybe . . . but I seem to remember something about that area of town. What was it? If only I could remember. . . ."

Gabriela got that faraway look in her eye that appears when she's working on a case. I knew we wouldn't be making any more small talk that day. I sighed and finished folding the papers in silence.

The next day we read that the fire marshal had ruled the fire an accident. He said it was an electrical fire caused by faulty wiring in the building that was closest to being finished. The fire had spread quickly because of all the building materials sitting around.

"See, Gabriela? No mystery. It was just an accident," I said as I waved the paper in front of her. She had a weird look on her face. At first I thought she was mad, but then she smiled and said, "Let's do our route."

That evening she dragged me to the library to check the microfilm of old issues of the *Tribune*. When I asked why we were there, she had that same look my cat had when he stared at our parakeet.

"I remembered what was important about the part of town where the fire was," she said. "That's the area where they're planning on building the new sports complex. See?" She pulled up an article on the screen.

CITY NARROWS CHOICE TO CITY HEIGHTS AREA

City planner Marilyn Brooks announced yesterday that the city has moved forward in its plans for the new Ted Williams Sports Complex. She said that the City Heights section of the city has been chosen as the best area for the complex because of its central location and easy freeway access. The commission continues to seek the exact site for the complex, but Brooks stated that three specific blocks were under consideration.

Gabriela had a gleam in her eye. "Tomorrow," she said, "I need to go interview some people in City Heights. And then I think I'll make a trip downtown."

"Why?" I asked. I was getting good at being Watson.

"You'll see," she replied.

The next afternoon I started to worry when Gabriela didn't show up to help fold the newspapers. Her mother was just getting home from work when I had them all folded and ready to deliver.

"What do you mean, Elena? She wasn't here when you came over?"

"No," I said. "You don't know where she is?"

"She told me the two of you were going to look at the burned-out apartment buildings."

"She didn't invite me," I said.

Her mother stared off down the street. "Well, don't worry," she said. "I'm sure she's okay."

I ended up doing the whole route myself. At each corner I stopped, hoping to see Gabriela zipping toward me on her bike. But I couldn't find her anywhere.

I was really relieved when I turned the corner toward home and spotted her bike on the balcony of their apartment. I ran up the stairs and knocked on the door.

"Come in, Elena," her mother shouted. "I was just about to find out where Gabriela has been all this time."

"I'm so glad to see you," I said.

"Sorry about the route," she told me, "but I had some important business to attend to."

"What sort of business?" her mother asked sternly.

"Well, after I asked several people in City Heights some questions, I figured out my apartment fire case! I just had to go to City Hall to check on something."

"City Hall? *Amiga loca*!" I said.

"It didn't make sense to me that those apartments were never finished. I mean, the guy building them—Mr. Fredericks—is one of the richest guys in the city! When I found that *Tribune* article about the location of the sports complex, something clicked in my brain. I wanted to find out when the construction on the apartment buildings stopped. So I asked some people who live around there, and guess what? The work stopped just before the article was published!"

I still had no idea where Gabriela was going with this.

"Then I remembered seeing something in that gossip column—you know, the one Miss Whispers writes. It was just a little piece about seeing Mr. Fredericks and Ms. Brooks eating lunch together at some fancy restaurant. Miss Whispers said they had their heads together, talking very seriously. She was trying to suggest they were having a romance!"

"Yes?" said Gabriela's mother. She was starting to look really interested now. I myself still wasn't following the clues.

"Well, I started thinking that what they were having was an illegal discussion about the site of that sports complex. So, I went to City Hall and got the minutes from the most recent meeting of the zoning commission."

Gabriela's eyes were really bright now, and a dull light was coming on in my brain.

"One of the motions that they passed was to change the zoning of the lots where Mr. Fredericks's apartment buildings were from residential to business. And—" she paused dramatically, "—that meeting was held three days before the fire!"

"Are you saying. . . ."

"*Sí*, Mama. Mr. Fredericks may be rich, but he's also greedy. Not only did he figure out how to sell his property to the city, but he also figured out how to collect insurance on the apartments. He's a crook!"

"And an arsonist," I added, happy to finally understand what Gabriela was talking about.

A few days later Gabriela's mom gave us the good news. When she told the police chief Gabriela's ideas about the fire, he decided that there was enough evidence to investigate the matter further. He said they would question both Mr. Fredericks and Ms. Brooks.

"Sherlock!" I said. "I can't believe you actually solved the mystery!"

"We're very proud of you, Gabriela," her mother said. "That's the kind of detective work that we need on the police force."

"*Muchas gracias*," she said, with a big smile.

I looked at her and asked, "Do you think you'll need an assistant when you're a world-famous detective?"

"Definitely, Watson. Every good detective needs help now and then, even if it's just to deliver her share of newspapers!"

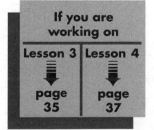

If you are working on

Lesson 3	Lesson 4
⬇	⬇
page 35	page 37

Reviewing *Drawing Conclusions*

A. Read "Gabriela's Game" on pages 31-34. As you read, use clues from the story and your own knowledge and experience to draw conclusions about what you are reading. Write your ideas in the wide margins. Use this information on the chart below to help you analyze how you drew one of your conclusions.

Details from the Selection

My Thoughts and Experiences

+

CONCLUSION

B. How does Elena feel about having Gabriela for a friend? Give reasons for your conclusion.

_____

_____

_____

_____

_____

_____

_____

_____

_____

_____

Testing Drawing Conclusions

A. Read each passage below. On the lines that follow, draw a conclusion based on details in the story and your own experience. Then write which story details and personal experience helped you draw your conclusion.

1. Marshal plays guitar in a band. One night while she is performing, she notices a man sitting alone in the front of the hall. She gets the feeling that something odd is happening. Every few minutes he glances at the door. She starts to forget the chords of the song she is playing.

What conclusion can you draw about Marshal's feelings? Explain your response.

_____

_____

2. As the band is playing its last song, the man gets up and runs out of the auditorium. Suddenly, brakes screech and horns honk. Everyone runs outside. Working her way through the crowd, Marshal finds a smashed saxophone and a shoe with blood on it.

What conclusion can you draw about the saxophone and shoe? Explain your response.

_____

_____

3. A police officer arrives on the scene. Marshal thinks about telling him about the mysterious man, but the man has disappeared. She's sure he's involved. But how? She turns to walk back into the auditorium, and there he is.

What conclusion can you draw about the man? Explain your response.

_____

_____

B. Suppose you knew that the man in the story is a police officer. How would that knowledge affect the conclusions that you have drawn?

_____

_____

_____

To begin
Lesson 4

page
26

Reviewing *Problem and Solution*

A. Reread "Gabriela's Game" on pages 31-34. As you read, underline the parts of the story that help you understand its problem and solution. Use the story map below to organize your information.

Title _____ **Author** _____

Characters _____
_____

Setting _____
Time _____

PROBLEM _____
_____

Event _____

Event _____

Event _____

SOLUTION _____

B. Write the first paragraph of a newspaper story that explains the crime Gabriela uncovered and how she solved it. Include a headline to accompany the story.

_____
_____
_____
_____
_____

Testing Problem and Solution

A. Circle the letter of the true statement in each pair of statements below. On the lines that follow it, explain your choice.

1. a. The title refers to a new mystery game Gabriela read about in a newspaper.
   b. The title refers to a game played in the mind.

_____

_____

2. a. Elena is an important character because her questions give Gabriela a chance to show what she is thinking.
   b. Elena is an unimportant character whose life is made more exciting by her friend Gabriela.

_____

_____

3. a. Gabriela solves the problem by reading, talking, thinking, and remembering.
   b. Gabriela is only able to solve the problem after getting help from her mother, who is a police detective.

_____

_____

B. How might the problem and solution in this story be different if Gabriela and Elena didn't deliver newspapers?

_____

_____

_____

_____

_____

_____

_____

_____

_____

Unit THREE

BECOMING AN ACTIVE READER

Good readers read **articles** to learn about something new or to add to their knowledge of a subject. They gather the facts they learn and add them to what they already know. Good readers then summarize as they read to make sure they understand the new information.

Using Skills and Strategies

Asking questions will help you **read nonfiction**. As you read articles and textbooks, you may ask: What do I already know about this topic? What does the title tell me? Are there subheadings that outline the article? What details does the author use to explain the topic?

Nonfiction writers often use bold or italic type to call attention to **key words**. You may ask: What do I know about the words set in bold or italic type? How does understanding these words help me understand the article?

In this unit, learning to **read nonfiction** and to understand **key words** will help you read articles and textbook chapters more actively.

The Article: The Writer's Voice

Writers often publish articles to give others a glimpse into their culture. They may present the wide variety of the culture's music or dance. They may also discuss issues important to their culture, like how new immigrants are adjusting to life in the United States. By telling people about their culture, writers help all cultures to know one another better.

Responding to Articles

Good readers use what they learn in their reading to increase their knowledge of the world. They may find, for example, that learning about one culture's music can help them understand the music from many cultures. Write your thoughts in the side margins as you read "Cuban Americans Today" and "The Beginnings of Art in Africa." Refer to these notes as you discuss the selections with your classmates.

Reading Nonfiction

Introducing Strategies

When good readers read **nonfiction**, they look at how the material is organized and what they might learn from it. An article or a textbook chapter usually has one topic stated in its title. Within the piece, additional information is usually organized into subtopics, which are often set off with subheads that are in boldfaced type. The subheads can serve as subtopics in an outline. Under each subtopic are details that support or explain it. The diagram below shows how articles and textbook chapters are often organized.

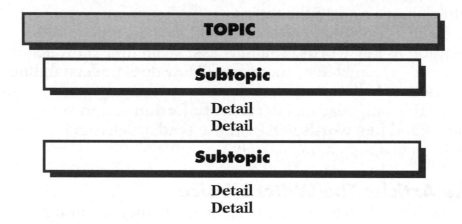

TOPIC

Subtopic

Detail
Detail

Subtopic

Detail
Detail

Reading Nonfiction

Read "Cuban Americans Today" and the sidenotes on pages 46-48. These notes show one reader's thoughts about how the information in the article is organized. After you have finished reading, complete the items below.

1. What did the reader learn about subheads? Use an example from the article.

_____

_____

2. List the details in the article that the reader found that explain or support the subhead.

_____

_____

Practicing Reading Nonfiction

A. Circle the letter of the item that best completes each statement below. Then, on the lines that follow, explain your answer.

1. The chapter begins with a brief description of the life of a Cuban American in order to
   a. show that many Cubans came to live in the United States.
   b. point out that women can become lawyers.
   c. give a personal glimpse of what it's like to be a Cuban American.
   d. point out that many Cuban Americans are anti-Castro.

   _____

   _____

2. The subtopic "The Second Havana" contains details that
   a. describe life in the Cuban neighborhoods of Miami.
   b. paint a detailed picture of Union City, New Jersey.
   c. describe what it's like to speak two languages.
   d. explain dating and chaperones.

   _____

   _____

3. Which detail does **not** support the subtopic "From Refugees to Citizens"?
   a. Cuban Americans recognize the power of voting.
   b. After the Bay of Pigs, many Cubans became U.S. citizens.
   c. Miami is called "the second Havana."
   d. Xavier Suárez is the first Cuban mayor of a major U.S. city.

   _____

   _____

B. On the lines below, list three additional things you would like to learn about Cuban Americans and their culture. List the three subheads you might expect to appear on these new sections.

   _____

   _____

   _____

Applying Reading Nonfiction

A. Read the excerpt below, which is from a U.S. history textbook. Then complete the items that follow it.

A VICIOUS CYCLE OF DEPENDENCE

Miners were not paid in United States currency but rather in paper money, or scrip, printed by the mine owners. The only place this scrip could be spent was in the company store, also owned by the mine owners. Prices there were high and miners were usually in debt to the store. The houses, too, were owned by the company, so if a miner fell ill, became unable to work, quit, or went out on strike, he lost not just his job but his home as well. Misfortune especially struck families of miners who were killed in the dangerous mines. Not only did they lose loved ones, but they lost their homes and livelihood with no compensation.

1. State the topic of this passage in your own words.

_____

_____

2. Give details from the passage that support or explain this topic.

_____

_____

_____

_____

B. Describe the "cycle" mentioned in the boldfaced head in the passage above. Then think of a title for the chapter from which this section might have been taken.

_____

_____

_____

_____

_____

_____

_____

To review
⬇
page
51

Key Words

| Lesson 6 | Introducing
page 43 | Practicing
page 44 | Applying
page 45 | Reviewing
page 53 | Testing
page 54 |

Introducing Strategies

Key words are words whose meanings readers must know in order to understand their reading. They may be technical terms, new words, or words specific to the subject. In nonfiction writing, readers can sometimes tell key words by how they look. For example, textbooks may use **boldfaced** type to call attention to key words. In addition, general terms that might not be familiar to the reader, as well as foreign words and phrases, may be printed in *italic* type and followed by their definitions.

Here's a strategy for identifying and defining key words.

DEFINING KEY WORDS			
Ask Yourself:	**Yes**	**/ No**	**If Yes:**
Is the key word printed in boldfaced or italic type?	☐	☐	Write the word.
Are there clues to the word's meaning in the text?	☐	☐	Write the clues.
Is a definition for the key word given in the text?	☐	☐	Write the definition.
How does understanding the key word help me understand the topic?			

Reading the Article

Reread "Cuban Americans Today" on pages 46-48. Circle any key words you find, and underline their definitions. Then complete the items below.

1. Write two key words you found and their definitions.

_____

_____

2. What term printed in italic type did you find? Write the term and its definition.

_____

_____

_____

Practicing Key Words

A. Read this passage and the statements that follow it. Fill in the bubble in front of any statement that is true. Explain your response on the lines below.

Historians think that the first people to live on the island arrived by **coracle***, a small boat made by covering a light wooden frame with waterproof material. These people probably knew how to chip flint into tools and to navigate, or steer their course, using the stars. Their earlier peregrinations, or journeys, probably led them as far west as the coast of Africa.*

○ **1.** The key word in the passage refers to boats and sailing.

_____

_____

○ **2.** To understand the information in the passage, readers must know the meaning of *navigate*.

_____

_____

○ **3.** Another meaning for *navigate* is "to guide from one point to another."

_____

_____

○ **4.** Another term for *peregrination* is "settle down."

_____

_____

B. Open a dictionary to any page and find two words you don't know. Use each one in a sentence that provides context clues to its definition.

_____

_____

_____

_____

_____

Applying Key Words

A. Read the passage below, then complete the items that follow it.

*Every group of people has its own **culture**—the customs, art, music, and everyday conveniences that belong to that group. More than one culture can exist at the same time and place—each with its own **mores**, or rules of behavior. For example, a ninth grader of Greek American ancestry may speak the language of his forebears, or ancestors, at home and eat traditional foods like dolmades, grape leaves stuffed with rice and spices, and baklava, a dessert made of layers of light pastry and honey, at meals with his family. At the same time, this same young man may be found wearing the latest U.S. fashions and sipping an orange soda at the mall with his friends from school.*

1. Find two key words in the excerpt and explain what these words tell you about the subject.

_____

_____

_____

2. From which of the following books was the excerpt probably taken: *Life in Present-Day America, Greek Gods and Heroes,* or *A Closer Look at Chicago's Neighborhoods*? Explain your choice.

_____

_____

_____

B. How does understanding the key words in this paragraph help you understand the entire paragraph?

_____

_____

_____

_____

_____

To review

page 53

Deborah Parks began her teaching career working with the children of migrant workers. While in graduate school, she taught ESOL students in the open admissions program of the City University of New York. She later taught in schools in the South Bronx and upstate New York. Today Deborah is a freelance writer and journalist. She continues to follow—and write about—the Latino children who form the Centro Mater Runners of Miami.

The title tells me what this chapter is about. I wonder what kinds of things I'll learn about Cuban Americans.

The notes in the margin show what one reader thought about how the information in the article is organized.

Cuban Americans Today

by Deborah A. Parks

Ana María Escagedo was one of the first children to attend the Centro Mater. Today she is a successful lawyer in Miami. Some of her earliest memories are of life in North Miami. "At home, we ate Cuban food, listened to Cuban music, and spoke Spanish. Today, we still speak Spanish at my parents' house." But when she became a teenager, some changes occurred. "I listened to rock-and-roll on the radio, while my parents listened to Latin music." When she started dating, her parents sent along a chaperone to supervise her behavior and that of her boyfriend. That was what they would have done in Cuba. "I didn't like that at all," said Ana María, laughing.

This is a story about one Cuban American. The difference between old and new customs is interesting.

I don't blame her. Having a chaperone sounds just awful.

In her work as a lawyer in Miami, Ana María Escagedo's ability to speak both Spanish and English is a great asset. "Our clients come from all over the Spanish-speaking world," she noted.

These details help me see Cuban Americans as real people.

What is it like to be among the first generation of Cuban Americans to grow up in the United States? "Great!" she exclaimed. "We have the chance to pick the best of both cultures."

Here's the first subhead. I think I'll stop here and look for others so I know what to expect from the whole article.

Diversity and Success

More than one million Cuban Americans live in the United States today. They are the third-largest Spanish-speaking group in the nation. Their backgrounds and experiences vary greatly. Their occupations range from factory workers to wealthy business owners.

Today, slightly less than 30 percent of all Cuban Americans are lawyers, doctors, engineers, university professors, school administrators and teachers, and businesspeople. The majority work at blue-collar trades. They have jobs as service workers, farmers, machine operators, and craftworkers. Ties among

Cuban Americans remain strong. Most Cuban American blue-collar workers have jobs in companies or agricultural businesses owned or managed by Cuban Americans.

Among Latino groups, Cuban Americans lead the way in income. In 1990, Cuban American families earned an average yearly income of $31,400. This figure was only slightly less than the $32,270 average yearly income of non-Latino white families.

In addition, more than 83 percent of all Cuban Americans aged 25 to 34 had graduated from high school. Within that same age group, over 24 percent had also completed four or more years of college.

The Second Havana

Like other Latino groups, Cuban Americans live in nearly every state of the Union. Union City, New Jersey, boasts the second-largest population of Cuban Americans in the nation after Miami. The more than 100,000 Cuban Americans there have brought new life to the neighborhoods in which they live. Cuban food stores, bakeries, and coffee shops line the streets.

But Miami continues to be the capital of Cuban America. Cuban Americans affectionately call the city "the second Havana." Today, more than 600,000 Cuban Americans—over 50 percent of all Cuban Americans, live in Dade County, where Miami is located. Since 1970, more Cuban Americans have moved into the Miami area than have moved out of it. This contrasts sharply with Puerto Ricans and Mexican Americans. They tend to spread out across the nation.

Cuban Americans have turned Miami into a Latin American boomtown. More than 250 **multinationals,** or companies with business operations in more than one nation, have opened headquarters there. Miami is located on the edge of the Caribbean basin. That and the city's strong Latino atmosphere have led Latin American business leaders to invest more than one billion dollars a year in the city.

From Refugees to Citizens

Since the failed Bay of Pigs invasion, more and more Cubans have become U.S. citizens. Cuban American voters have flexed their political muscle in recent years. They have sent the first Cuban Americans to Congress. In 1985, voters in Miami elected Xavier Suárez as the first Cuban American mayor of a major U.S. city.

◀ The information in this paragraph explains the subhead. It gives details that tell about both diversity and success.

◀ Cuban Americans seem to be successful in all fields. I like that they stick together and give jobs to their own people. My uncles sent my father money to bring us here from Vietnam, and they gave Mother a job when we got here.

◀ I know that Havana is in Cuba. Maybe this section will talk about where Cubans live in the United States.

◀ I was right. Cuban immigrants must feel comfortable moving to Miami. I bet it's easier to learn a new language and customs when you still have people nearby who know your first language and culture.

As you read, continue writing your own notes in the margins about how the information is organized in the article.

A Center of Latino Culture

The heart of the Spanish-speaking culture in Miami is Calle Ocho, or Eighth Street, in Little Havana. Here Cuban restaurants serve up heaping dishes of traditional Cuban foods such as *picadillo con arroz y huevos* (ground meat with rice and eggs). Newsstands are filled with newspapers and magazines written in Spanish. Older men play dominoes for hours in Antonio Macéo Park while they drink cups of thick Cuban coffee. Here and there, anti-Castro slogans and drawings streak the walls of buildings.

Yet, despite the strong Cuban presence, Calle Ocho is changing. Today, immigrants from all over Latin America head to Miami to start new lives in the United States.

Today, Calle Ocho is like Miami itself. It is a mix of Latino cultures. Perhaps one of the greatest contributions of Cuban Americans has been to open the doors of Miami to people from all over Latin America. In the 30 years in which Cuban Americans have made the city their home, they have helped turn Miami into what they proudly call the "Gateway of Latin America."

Looking Ahead

Since the huge immigration of Cubans to the United States in the late 1960s, the Cuban American community has shown more diversity. Settling into Miami, Union City, and several other cities, Cuban Americans have formed stable communities that are a mix of Cuban and U.S. traditions.

Since 1980, the number of Latino immigrants to the United States from Central America and the Dominican Republic has risen sharply. In the past decade, immigrants from these regions have passed Cubans as the largest group of refugees seeking economic or political shelter in the United States.

If you are working on

Lesson 5	Lesson 6
⬇	⬇
page 40	page 43

Helena St. Louis was born in Trinidad, an island off the coast of Venezuela. As a fabric designer, she printed fabrics that were sold mostly to tourists in local markets. She also taught art to children, passing on the rich heritage of her African ancestors. In the 1970s, she immigrated to Los Angeles. Although she is now retired, she still enjoys sharing her knowledge of African art.

The Beginnings of Art in Africa

by Helena St. Louis

As you read, write your own ideas in the margins about how the information in this article is organized.

Imagine yourself walking in the *Sahara*, the vast, desolate desert of northern Africa. You are surrounded only by sand, rocks, and heat. You come upon a rock formation. You try to sit down, but the rocks are too hot. Then you look a little closer and you see lines **engraved,** or cut, into the rock. At first you do not believe your eyes— someone has engraved an elephant into the rock. You look around and see many other animals. Who could have made these drawings? And when? Why would anyone engrave drawings of animals in the middle of the desert?

Africa's Oldest Picture Gallery

Some of the earliest examples of African art are found in the Sahara. Drawings of animals were engraved in the rock nearly 8,000 years ago. The **engravings,** or pictures cut into rock, were made long before the Sahara became a desert. The animals depicted in the engravings actually lived in the area at the time.

If you look closely at the engraving on this page, you will see that it is **realistic**, that it really looks like a group

of rabbits. The desert drawings are known for their realistic depictions of animals, including hippopotamuses, giraffes, ostriches, and rhinoceroses. Rock paintings and engravings of people and animals are also part of the Saharan picture gallery, although these are not as old as the first engravings of animals.

You might wonder why these drawings were made. But the reasons have been lost over time. However, these early artworks probably had religious importance to the people who made them. Even today, art and religion are important to many Africans.

Africa's Ancient Sculptures

Now imagine that you are at an *archaeological excavation*, a place where scientists are digging up old objects to learn about people who lived long ago. You are on the *Jos Plateau*, a high, flat region in central Nigeria. You have only a toothbrush to work with so that you don't damage the things you find. Then all of a sudden you notice what looks like a nose made out of clay. Excitedly you call the other workers over to look. You carefully brush away the earth to reveal a face. Eventually, you uncover a life-sized head of a person. Later, the experts determine that the age of the figure is 2500 years old. You have found a *Nok* sculpture made in 500 B.C. by a group of people called the *Nok*.

The sculpture on this page is an example of a Nok sculpture. Notice the large, triangular eyes, which are typical of the Nok heads. Also notice how the artist used line, shape, and texture to make the features of the face. It's hard to imagine that this sculpture was made so long ago.

Nok artists used **terracotta**, a type of baked clay, to make their sculptures. After forming the entire figure, head and body, the artist would **fire**, or bake, it in a large clay furnace. Today, few entire figures exist—in most cases, only the head has survived time.

If you are working on

Lesson 5	Lesson 6
⬇	⬇
page 51	page 53

Lesson 5	Introducing page 40	Practicing page 41	Applying page 42	Reviewing page 51	Testing page 52

Reviewing Reading Nonfiction

A. Read "The Beginnings of Art in Africa" on pages 49-50. Circle the boldfaced subheads and underline the details that support the topics named in these heads. Then use this information to complete the chart below.

TOPIC ______________________________

Subtopic ______________________________

Detail ______________________________

Detail ______________________________

Subtopic ______________________________

Detail ______________________________

Detail ______________________________

B. Imagine that people today created artworks similar to those described in this article. List the subheads that might apply to this topic. Write at least two details for each subhead.

____

____

____

____

____

____

____

____

____

____

____

____

Testing Reading Nonfiction

A. In each pair below, circle the letter of the item or items that are true. Then, on the lines provided, explain why you answered as you did.

1. a. One subtopic in "The Beginnings of Art in Africa" discusses the religious beliefs held by the artists.

   b. One subtopic in "The Beginnings of Art in Africa" talks about African Nok sculptures.

   _____

2. a. This article talks about two of the oldest forms of art in Africa.

   b. This article covers African art from its beginnings to the present day.

   _____

3. a. Details about the Sahara engravings help readers visualize, or picture, what these look like.

   b. Details about the Sahara engravings help readers imagine what it would be like to cross the Sahara.

   _____

4. a. Details under the subhead "Africa's Ancient Sculptures" provide information about how these sculptures were made.

   b. Details under the subhead "Africa's Ancient Sculptures" provide information about size and style of the sculptures.

   _____

B. Imagine someone asked you to explain a topic you know about. Organize your information on the lines below in outline form. Be sure to include three subheads and supporting details.

_____

_____

_____

_____

_____

To begin
Lesson 6

page
43

Reviewing Key Words

A. Reread the article "The Beginnings of Art in Africa" on pages 49-50. Look for key words printed in boldfaced type and other important terms printed in italics. Record your findings on the chart below.

DEFINING KEY WORDS		
Ask Yourself:	**Yes / No**	**If Yes:**
Is the key word printed in boldfaced or italic type?	☐ ☐	Write the word. _____
Are there clues to the word's meaning in the text?	☐ ☐	Write the clues. _____ _____
Is a definition for the key word given in the text?	☐ ☐	Write the definition. _____ _____
How does understanding the key word help me understand the topic? _____		

B. Helena St. Louis enjoys teaching others about the art that is part of her African heritage. What would you like to teach others about your heritage? Jot down your ideas below. Be sure to include at least two key words that will allow your audience to better understand your information.

_____

_____

_____

_____

_____

_____

_____

_____

Testing Key Words

A. Read the passage below. Then read it a second time and write the word that best fills each blank. Pay special attention to key words and specialized terms.

HUMOR IN PRESENT-DAY AMERICA

1. Laughs
   Tears
   Audiences

2. boredom
   humor
   comparison

3. remake
   parody
   skit

4. detectives
   lampoons
   events

5. sarcasm
   skit
   roman a clef

6. novels
   jibes
   skits

_____ (1) can be gotten in many ways. One way seems well suited to television—the **parody**, a humorous skit based on and imitating another serious work. Of course, the audience has to know what's being **lampooned**, or made fun of. The _____ (2) of a parody lies in comparing it to the real thing. For example, the cartoon "Miami Mice" is a _____ (3) of the TV series "Miami Vice."

The printed word can also be amusing. Serious works may contain an occasional **jibe**, a witty or sarcastic remark, for a humorous touch. Or a writer may devote an entire book to humor. A *roman a clef* is a novel in which fictional characters and happenings resemble real people and _____ (4). In a fictional story of her own life, novelist Nora Ephron creates a _____ (5) full of laughs as well as tears. And there are always the humor magazines. Few public figures and events are spared the _____ (6) of publications like *Mad* or *National Lampoon*.

B. List three words or terms that helped you complete section A. Write a definition for each one.

_____

_____

_____

_____

Unit FOUR

BECOMING AN ACTIVE READER

Active readers are critical readers. They read **articles** to look for ideas they can use in their own lives. They check the facts they find against their own personal experience. If the facts fit and can help them, they accept the facts as true.

Using Skills and Strategies

Identifying **comparisons** and **contrasts** will help you see an author's ideas clearly. You may ask: What do these two things have in common? In what ways are they different? How do these comparisons help me understand the article?

Finding the **main idea** and **details** in an article will help you analyze the writer's argument. You may ask: What is the most important point in the article? What sentence tells me this? What details support this main idea? What do I know that supports or challenges the main idea?

In this unit, identifying **comparisons and contrasts** and finding **main ideas and details** will help you read articles more actively.

Reading Articles

Good readers rely on articles for new information. They read to learn and even to improve their lives. If you read an article and need to remember facts, it will help if you take notes, summarize, or make an outline of the article's points. If the article is in a book or magazine of your own, you might underline key points and write your thoughts and feelings in the margins.

Responding to Articles

Good readers often respond to articles by analyzing the information presented. They learn key facts and decide how these facts can help them understand other topics. Jot down notes in the side margins as you read "The Facts About Skin Cancer" and "Estonia Returns to Life." Writing sidenotes will help you remember important points in the articles. Use these notes as you discuss the articles with your classmates.

Compare and Contrast

| Lesson 7 | Introducing page 56 | Practicing page 57 | Applying page 58 | Reviewing page 70 | Testing page 71 |

Introducing Strategies

One way authors structure nonfiction articles is by **comparing and contrasting** information. Comparing shows qualities that two people, places, ideas, or events have in common. Contrasting tells what is different about the two items. The diagram below shows how this works. The outside section of each oval shows characteristics that are specific to that item. The section in which the ovals overlap shows characteristics that the two have in common.

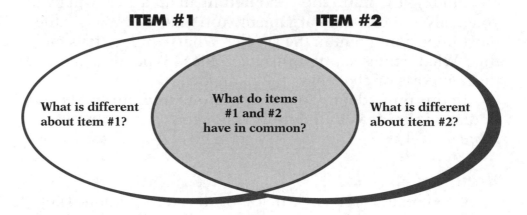

ITEM #1   **ITEM #2**

What is different about item #1?

What do items #1 and #2 have in common?

What is different about item #2?

Reading the Article

Read "The Facts About Skin Cancer" and the sidenotes on pages 62-65. These notes show one reader's responses to the comparisons and contrasts in the article. After you have finished reading, use these sidenotes to complete the items below.

1. On the lines below, write one example of comparing and contrasting that the reader found in the article.

_____

_____

2. Explain the similarities and differences of the items.

_____

_____

Practicing Compare and Contrast

A. Read the items below and explain what is being compared or contrasted in each one.

1. Tanned skin is unhealthy; untanned skin can be healthy.

_____

_____

2. Today the ozone layer is letting in more harmful rays than it has in the past.

_____

_____

3. Getting a sunburn that blisters as a child or teen can make a person twice as likely to get skin cancer.

_____

_____

4. Exposing your skin to a sunlamp is like exposing your skin to the sun.

_____

_____

5. Sunbathing at noon is much worse for the skin than sunbathing at 4 P.M.

_____

_____

B. Write three short rules for good health in the sun. In each rule, use comparing, contrasting, or both to make clear the reasons for your rules.

_____

_____

_____

_____

_____

_____

_____

Applying Compare and Contrast

A. Read the following paragraph from a science textbook. Then answer the questions that follow it.

A human eye is like a camera. Both have a lens that focuses rays of light. In the eye, these rays fall on the retina, which can be compared to the film in a camera. The amount of light entering the eye is controlled by the muscles in the iris, the colored area that surrounds the pupil. Some cameras have ways to control the amount of light admitted. Their apertures, or openings, look a little like an expanding and contracting iris. Of course, living eyes are much different from cameras. One difference is that eyes contain a watery fluid, called the aqueous humor, *while cameras are dry inside. Another is that the surface of the eye is constantly being cleaned by tears. Camera lenses, in contrast, can collect dirt and dust that must be wiped away.*

1. According to the article, in what ways are eyes and cameras alike?

_____

_____

_____

2. In what ways are eyes and cameras different?

_____

_____

_____

B. Write two facts you learned about suntanning in "The Facts About Skin Cancer." Then write two statements in which you contrast what you know now with what you thought before you read.

_____

_____

To review
⬇
page 70

_____

_____

_____   _____

_____

_____

Main Idea and Details

Introducing Strategies

The **main idea** is the central, or most important, point that a writer makes. Main ideas can be stated directly, as they usually are in textbook articles. In essays, sometimes main ideas are implied, which means that readers must determine the main idea from the information given.

In nonfiction writing, the main idea is often stated in the opening paragraph or paragraphs. Each subsequent paragraph has its own main idea which supports the central idea of the article. Writers use **details** to support or provide evidence for their main ideas. The diagram below shows how details support the main idea.

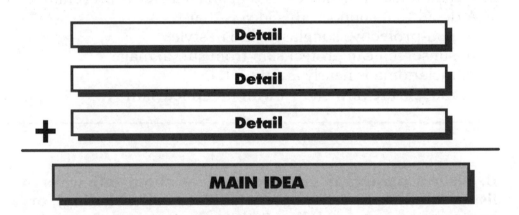

```
        ┌──────────────────────────────┐
        │           Detail             │
        └──────────────────────────────┘
        ┌──────────────────────────────┐
        │           Detail             │
        └──────────────────────────────┘
   +    ┌──────────────────────────────┐
        │           Detail             │
        └──────────────────────────────┘
   ─────────────────────────────────────
        ┌──────────────────────────────┐
        │          MAIN IDEA           │
        └──────────────────────────────┘
```

Reading the Article

Reread "The Facts About Skin Cancer" on pages 62-65. As you read, underline the main idea of the article. Circle details that support it. Then use this information to answer the questions below.

1. What is the main idea of this article?

_____

2. List three details that support this main idea.

_____

_____

_____

Practicing Main Idea and Details

A. Circle the letter in front of the phrase that best completes each statement. Then, on the lines that follow, explain your choice.

1. In one paragraph of this essay, readers learn that a major cause of the rise in skin cancer is forgetfulness. This idea is supported by
   a. the fact that there is a hole in the ozone layer.
   b. pointing out that more people are spending time outdoors and not remembering to apply sunscreen.
   c. explaining that UV rays are ultraviolet.
   d. telling the tragic story of a young lifeguard.

   _____

   _____

2. A main idea of the article is that skin cancer is preventable. A detail that supports this idea is that
   a. non-protective sunglasses are in style.
   b. sunscreen can protect skin from sun damage.
   c. melanoma is nearly always fatal.
   d. models are now shown with untanned skin.

   _____

   _____

B. Write a paragraph giving your ideas about safe ways to listen to music or enjoy sports (such as rollerblading), or how to eat a balanced diet. Write a sentence stating your main idea, and include details that support it.

   _____

   _____

   _____

   _____

   _____

   _____

   _____

   _____

Applying Main Idea and Details

A. Read the following paragraph from a social studies textbook. Then find the main idea and the supporting details and write them on the lines below.

Did you know that when the Constitution of the United States was first approved, it was missing something important? The Bill of Rights, which contained the first 10 amendments to the U.S. Constitution, was added in 1791. These amendments gave citizens many important rights. One was the right to religious freedom. Another right guaranteed free speech. Freedom of assembly, or of meeting together peacefully, was also guaranteed. The right to a fair trial was also included in the Bill of Rights.

Main idea: _____

Details: _____

_____

_____

_____

B. Write a paragraph about a right that you think is especially important. Be sure to include at least three details to support your main idea.

_____

_____

_____

_____

_____

_____

_____

_____

_____

_____

_____

To review

↓

page 72

Kristi Jogis has a master's degree in Public Health. She works as a writer and researcher for Health & Education Communication Consultants in Redwood City, California. She is committed to lowering health risks among young people. She hopes the information below, which was written for a health textbook, will lead teens to protect their skin from the dangers of sunbathing.

The Facts About Skin Cancer

by Kristi Jogis

The notes in the margin show the comparisons and contrasts that one reader found in this article.

Most people enjoy being out in the sun. It reminds them of summer and having a good time. While being out in the sun can be fun, it can also be dangerous to your health. Your risk of **skin cancer** increases if you do not shield your skin from the sun.

There sure is a difference between the way people think today about tanning and the way they used to think. ▶ Doctors say that there is no such thing as a healthy tan. Today, people are becoming more aware of this fact. Models who used to bake themselves in the sun are now shown with "natural" or "untanned" skin.

Nevertheless, some people still insist on sunbathing. Many do not even use sunscreen to protect their skin from the sun. The fact remains that too much sun can kill you—even at a young age. If that sounds hard to believe, think about this true story: Mike was a lifeguard in California. He spent seven years in a row in the hot sun, guarding people's lives. He died of skin cancer when he was only 27 years old.

Skin Cancer Is on the Rise

The number of people who contract skin cancer increases each year. In the early 1990s, more than 6,000 people died each year of this disease. At least half of the most serious skin cancer cases occur in people between 15 and 50 years of age.

The details in this paragraph are frightening. I'm in almost as much danger as my parents are. ▶ There are two main reasons for the increase in skin cancer. One has to do with **ozone** loss. High above the earth is a layer of ozone. This gas protects the earth from the sun's **ultraviolet (UV) rays**. A few years ago, sun experts found a large hole in this ozone layer. UV rays can come through this hole. Too much UV light can cause

The earth still has an ozone layer that keeps out harmful rays, but now it has holes in it. That makes getting a tan even more dangerous. ▶ skin cancer. Yet, many people still go out in the sun without protection. The other reason for new cases of skin cancer is forgetfulness. Many sports-minded Americans are spending more and more time outdoors. Each time they go outside, even during a cloudy day, they should apply sunscreen. Yet, for many, this is a good health habit that seems hard to develop. Children should be taught to do this from an early age. Doctors tell us that most skin cancers start in childhood. Getting a sunburn that blisters as a child or teen can make a person twice as likely to get skin cancer.

How Sun Damages Skin

Skin is damaged by the sun's ultraviolet rays, which kill skin cells. There are two types of ultraviolet rays: **UVA** and **UVB**. UVB rays, often called the "burning" rays, go through the top layer of skin and cause painful sunburns which can lead to skin cancer. The longer UVA rays, called "tanning" or "aging" rays, go much deeper into the skin layer and break down the tissue that holds it together.

◀ The rays are alike because they both come from the sun. They are different because they damage different layers of the skin.

When a person gets a tan, his or her skin is making a brown substance called **melanin**. This is the skin's defense against the damage caused by the sun. Having a tan or a sunburn is only the first sign of skin damage. The long-term effects can include early wrinkling and skin cancer.

Artificial Tanning

Some people want a tan so much that they try to get one without the sun. One way to do that is by using a tanning salon. Some of these salons claim that exposure to sunlamps is safer than exposure to the sun. However, experts say that sunlamps cause the same damage as the sun does: skin aging, skin cancer, and eye damage.

◀ Tanning in a salon seems to be just as damaging as sunbathing is.

Tanning creams or "bronzers" are used by people who fear the effects of the sun but want to look tanned. These products contain dyes that make the skin brown. Most doctors think these products are safe to use. The main problem with bronzers is that people who use them often think they can be in the sun safely. Yet, most of these bronzers do not contain sunscreen.

Now write your own notes that make comparisons and contrasts about the information in the rest of the article.

One more fake tanning device is the tanning pill. Tanning pills contain food dyes that can turn the skin orange and may have other harmful side effects. Experts believe that these pills are not safe to use. Most are no longer sold.

The Three Types of Skin Cancer

One type of skin cancer is called **basal-cell carcinoma**. This is the most common type of skin cancer. It affects the top layer of the skin. The signs vary greatly. The cancer might be a reddish spot that tends to ooze, bleed, and crust over. It might be a pink or white bump. It might be a smooth red spot with a hollow or depression in the middle. In general, any sore that keeps crusting and does not heal should be checked by a doctor.

The next most common type of skin cancer is called **squamous-cell carcinoma**. This type tends to appear as a pink lump with a dent in the center. Basal-cell and squamous-cell cancers tend not to spread to other parts of the body.

The worst type of skin cancer is called **melanoma,** which often starts with a mole that changes color or shape. This type of cancer often spreads to other parts of the body. If it is not treated early, it is almost always fatal. A doctor treats skin cancer by either scraping off the diseased sore with a knife or by freezing it off.

Prevention: What You Can Do To Avoid Skin Cancer

Fortunately, there are many things you can do to avoid skin cancer. First, always use a sunscreen. This is an easy and cheap way to take care of your health. Doctors say that more than 80 percent of skin cancers could be avoided if people used a sunscreen every day. They encourage young people to make it a habit, like brushing their teeth.

There are many types of sunscreen available for all skin types. Some are made for athletes. Others are made for teens with problem skin. Doctors say that a sunscreen with an **SPF** (sun protective factor) of 15 is best for most people. An SPF of 15 means that the skin will be protected from sun damage 15 times longer than it would be if no sunscreen were used.

You can also shield your skin from the sun by wearing protective clothing. Experts say that 85 percent of skin cancers occur on the head, face, neck, and the back of the hand. For this reason, it is a good idea to wear long sleeves and a hat when you plan to be out in the sun for any length of time.

One thing that many people forget is how the sun damages their eyes. Too much sunlight can cause **cataracts**, a disease that results in a clouding of the eyes. In some cases, people have gone blind from too much sun. Wearing sunglasses while outdoors is very important. Small sunglasses may be in style, but they do not always protect your eyes. Look for glasses that are large and dark enough to keep eyes covered and protected. Don't worry about cost. Even low-cost sunglasses often have a sticker on them stating the amount of UV rays they shield.

Another way to protect your skin and eyes is to avoid being in the sun during the peak (hottest) hours: between 10:00 in the morning and 2:00 in the afternoon. Use this simple rule: If your shadow is shorter than you are, stay out of the sun.

One other healthy habit to develop is to check the skin all over your body once a month. If you notice a change, such as a new sore or a change in a mole, see a doctor right away. Paying attention to early warning signs can help you minimize the damage skin cancer can do.

Remember, skin cancer is one disease you can help to prevent by your actions. Make healthy habits designed to protect your skin a part of your daily routine. Certainly, you don't want to deny yourself "fun in the sun." Just remember to protect your skin so you can continue having that fun.

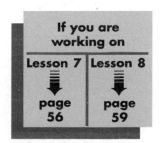

If you are working on

Lesson 7	Lesson 8
⬇	⬇
page 56	page 59

Estonia Returns to Life

by Elin Toona Gottschalk

As you read, make notes in the margins about life in Estonia before and after communism. Think about the comparisons and contrasts you find.

In August 1991, the world watched as communism ended in the Soviet Union. To Western eyes, it seemed as though half of the peoples on earth had been let out of prison. They gathered in the streets to celebrate their freedom. One by one, the once-independent nations took back the names that had been wiped off world maps since the end of World War II. Among them were the Baltic states of Estonia, Latvia, and Lithuania. Estonia is the smallest of the three Baltic states. On August 20, 1991, it regained its independence from the Soviet Union. So ended 52 years of Communist rule. As you read this article, think about what it would be like to live in Estonia when its independence was restored.

Ancient History

Estonia has a rich history dating to the Stone Age. Myths and legends of ancient times help us understand Estonian culture. Often, poetry was used to tell these stories. One poem containing 19,023 verses tells of the struggles and adventures of "Kalevipoeg" (Son of Kalev), a mythical Estonian ruler. Estonian folklore also includes stories about nature. This is not surprising since Estonia has 1,400 lakes and thousands of acres of forests. One myth about how the world was created came from a combination of shamanism, the worship of nature, and totemism, ancestor-animal worship. This myth says that the earth came from the egg of a wondrous bird. The Milky Way came from a giant tree. As is true for all ancient civilizations, information about Estonia's beginnings is limited to what archaeologists unearth and what historians piece together from written records. Think about what people can learn from earlier civilizations.

Before Soviet Occupation

Since ancient times Estonia has been ruled by German, Danish, Swedish, and Russian conquerors. The interest in the area has always been due to its location. On one side of Estonia is the Gulf of Finland. On the other side is the mostly ice-free Baltic Sea. This makes Estonia a gateway between Europe and Asia.

During the period 800 A.D. to 1270 A.D., Estonia was part of a great trade route. This route connected Scandinavia and the Middle Eastern centers of the Byzantine Empire. At that time, the traveling merchants who used the trade route were called Variags—or Vikings, as they are known in the Western world. Estonians prospered during this period by raiding settlements in Denmark and Sweden. In 1187, for example, a group of Estonians wiped out the major trading fort of Sigtuna in Sweden. The Estonians earned a bad reputation from these acts, which proved to be their downfall. In 1193, the Pope called for a Crusade against the "Baltic heathens." Religious armies carrying swords in one hand and crosses in the other swept through the Baltic lands. By 1227, the Estonians were conquered. Their land became a German colony named Livonia.

The Germans soon lost interest in defending Livonia. It took too much work to protect the country. The area continued to be desirable, and many countries wanted to control it. The Germans were followed by Danes, then Swedes, then Germans, then Russians, until 1917. That year marked the beginning of the Bolshevik Revolution in

Russia. Estonia was under Russian control at this time. The czar had allowed the area to govern itself, and the people were prospering. Therefore, they viewed the Revolution as their chance to regain independence.

Brief Independence

During the Bolshevik Revolution, Russia remained in control of Estonia. However, the Germans tried to re-occupy the country. It was a period of chaos, so the time was right for Estonians to take back control of their land. On August 25, 1917, Estonians made known their desire to become independent. The statement was made by Jaan Tonisson in a paper called a "Diet." Both Germany and Russia denied the declaration. Fighting continued until February 24, 1918, when Estonia firmly declared itself an independent republic. It was to remain independent for 20 years.

Throughout its 20 years of independence, Estonia prospered. It was admitted to the League of Nations, and soon became known as a country that treated all of its people fairly. How can you tell if a country treats its people fairly?

The Soviet Occupation

Estonia's independence lasted from February 1918 until August 1939. During World War II, Russia and Germany were locked in a struggle to be the most powerful force in the world. By 1939, Hitler's Nazi German troops were closing in on Russia. However, Stalin, the Russian leader, was still powerful enough to try to bargain for what was left of Europe. On August 23, 1939, the Non-Aggression Pact between Nazi Germany and Communist Russia was signed. A secret part of the treaty stated that the Baltic states and Poland would be divided between the two powers. Finland, Estonia, and Latvia were given to the Soviets. Lithuania and half of Poland went to Germany. The countries were supposed to be used as military bases. However, the Soviets quickly took over Estonia completely. From July 1940 until September 1941, the Soviets claimed to be "liberating," or freeing the Estonian workers. Yet, during those 14 months, Estonia lost 60,000 citizens. These people were either forced to leave the country or were killed for disagreeing with the Soviets. In one night alone (June 13, 1941), 10,200 Estonians were executed.

In 1941, Estonia came under German control when the Soviets were forced out. From August 1941 through

September 1944, Germany remained in control. As Germany began losing the war, Estonians panicked. They feared the return of the Communists and the terror they would bring. Many people fled. Those with boats went to Sweden. Others fled south through borders left open by the retreating Germans. When the war ended, the Soviets did control Estonia again. This time, Estonia was erased from the map, becoming instead part of the Soviet Union. Estonian farms were taken over by the government. All private business was forbidden. Protest and other forms of self-expression were illegal. Many Estonians were forced to leave the country and Soviet citizens were brought in. By 1991, only 65 percent of the people living in the area were native Estonians. Why do you think the Soviets treated Estonia in this way?

A New Independence

As you might have heard on the news, what started as the Bolshevik Revolution of 1917 ended with the August Coup of 1991. Estonia became independent once again. Yet, few could really understand what this meant. Three generations of Estonians had lived under tight Communist control. Thirty-five percent of the population was not Estonian. Many of the Communists were hostile about the new state of independence. Despite these problems, Estonia moved quickly ahead of other ex-Soviet Union areas. By the end of 1992, it had a stable government and its own money called the Kroon. It had also become a member of the United Nations.

Since independence, Estonians have delighted in doing many things that were not allowed under Soviet rule. Music and folklore festivals are frequently held. Estonian culture is celebrated at these events. Books are being written and printed without censorship. Education and technology are being brought up to modern standards. The economy is being brought back to life. Estonians believe their future is bright. They like to use these words: "Elagu Eesti! Long Live Estonia!"

If you are working on

Lesson 7	Lesson 8
↓	↓
page 70	page 72

Reviewing Compare and Contrast

A. Read "Estonia Returns to Life" on pages 66-69. This textbook article describes the country of Estonia at several points in its history. As you read, make notes in the margins about how the country remains the same and how it is different at each of these points. Then use the diagram below to organize your information.

ESTONIA BEFORE 1991   **ESTONIA AFTER 1991**

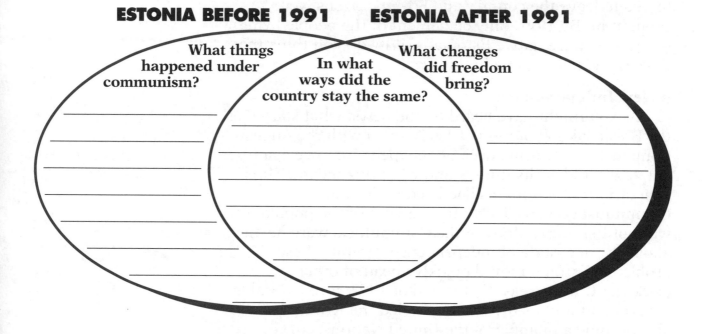

B. In what ways is this school year different from the last one? In what ways is it the same? In the space below, make a diagram like the one above that shows these similarities and differences.

Testing Compare and Contrast

A. Read each group of sentences below, then fill in the bubble that tells what is being compared. On the line below, explain your choice.

1. During the Bolshevik Revolution, Russia remained in control of Estonia. However, the Germans tried to reoccupy the country. It was a period of chaos, so the time was right for Estonians to take back control of their land.

○ the political climate
○ German and Russian domination
○ Estonians' attitude toward Germany and Russia

_____

2. From July 1940 until September 1941, the Soviets claimed to be "liberating," or freeing, the Estonian workers. Yet, during those 14 months, Estonia lost 60,000 citizens. These people were either forced to leave the country or were killed for disagreeing with the Soviets.

○ treatment of people
○ changes in borders
○ length of time

_____

3. Estonia moved quickly ahead of other ex-Soviet Union areas. By the end of 1992, it had a stable government and its own money called the Kroon. It had also become a member of the United Nations.

○ ancient and modern governments
○ Soviet and German rule
○ development of newly independent areas of the Soviet Union

_____

B. Think of two places you know well. Write three things about them that are alike and three things that are different.

_____

_____

_____

_____

To begin
Lesson 8

↓

page
59

Reviewing Main Idea and Details

A. Reread "Estonia Returns to Life" on pages 66-69. As you read, underline the main point the writer is making. Circle the details that support this point. The diagram below will help you organize your findings.

Detail _____

Detail _____

+ Detail _____

_____

MAIN IDEA _____
_____

B. Write a statement about a form of independence that you feel is particularly important. (For example, you might mention choosing friends, wearing the clothes you like, or listening to a certain type of music.) List two or three details that support your main idea.

_____
_____
_____
_____
_____
_____
_____
_____

Testing Main Idea and Details

A. Read each of the paragraphs below. Underline the sentence that has the main idea. Circle the sentences that give details to support the main idea. On the lines below, explain your choice.

1. The Peace Corps chooses American men and women from large numbers of applicants. The minimum age is 18, and there is no upper age limit. People who wish to work in the Peace Corps fill out a detailed application. The Peace Corps also uses letters of recommendation from teachers, employers, and friends in selecting volunteers.

_____

_____

_____

2. The Peace Corps carefully trains those selected as volunteers. The training lasts from 8 to 14 weeks. It usually takes place in the host country, or country where the volunteer will serve. Volunteers study the language and learn the customs of the people in their host country.

_____

_____

_____

B. Write a paragraph about a job that interests you. Circle details that support your main idea.

_____

_____

_____

_____

_____

_____

_____

_____

_____

_____

BECOMING AN ACTIVE READER

Reading an **essay** is like having a conversation with someone. The writer's words and the reader's thoughts make up the conversation. When active readers find that their ideas differ from the writer's, they consider the evidence and decide either to change their mind or to stick with their own ideas.

Using Skills and Strategies

Asking questions will help you understand the **author's viewpoint** as you read. You may ask: What facts does the writer present? What are the writer's feelings about the topic? Where in the essay can I find these feelings? How can I relate this viewpoint to my own experience?

All readers find unfamiliar words in their reading. Using **context clues**, or looking at the other words and ideas in the sentence, can help you define these new words. You may ask: What does the rest of this sentence mean? What clues can I use to guess this word's meaning? What meaning for this word makes sense in this sentence?

In this unit, determining the **author's viewpoint** and using **context clues** will help you read essays actively.

The Essay: The Writer's Voice

Essays from many cultures tell us about people's thoughts and feelings. Writers may show us various points of view from other cultures as well as from our own culture. In learning about what people in other cultures are thinking, we can learn that we have much in common with people all over the world.

Responding to Essays

When they read essays, good readers look for new points of view that can add to their understanding. Jot down your reactions in the side margins as you read "What's in a Name?" and "Little Bighorn: A Native American Perspective." These sidenotes will help you have your own discussion with the writers. Refer to your notes as you discuss these essays with your classmates.

Author's Viewpoint

| Lesson 9 | Introducing page 75 | Practicing page 76 | Applying page 77 | Reviewing page 86 | Testing page 87 |

Introducing Strategies

Authors write essays to give their **viewpoint**, or position, on a topic. Good readers look for the author's viewpoint by considering the thoughts and feelings the author expresses and the facts he or she chooses. For example, Monica, a school newspaper editor, might write, "Ninth-graders are responsible enough to be allowed to eat their lunch outside." This is her feeling on the topic.

She might also write, "Studies show that ninth-graders can be trusted to follow rules." This fact supports her feeling. Her feelings and this fact support her viewpoint that ninth-graders should be allowed to eat lunch outside.

The chart below shows how to find an author's viewpoint.

Reading the Essay

Read "What's in a Name?" and the sidenotes on pages 81-83. The sidenotes show what one reader thought about the author's viewpoint. Use these notes to complete the items below.

1. Write one fact and one feeling that the reader found.

_____

_____

2. What does the reader think is the author's viewpoint?

_____

_____

Practicing Author's Viewpoint

A. For each item, decide whether the quotation contains facts, the author's thoughts and feelings, or both kinds of information. Circle the letter of your answer. On the lines that follow, explain your choice.

1. "I was in junior high in Queens, New York."
   a. personal thoughts and feelings
   b. facts
   c. both **a** and **b**

   _____

   _____

2. "While others shed their 'slave names,' I kept my name, Linda Michelle Baron. I saw it as part of my own history."
   a. personal thoughts and feelings
   b. facts
   c. both **a** and **b**

   _____

3. "We of African descent should never forget what our people have survived."
   a. personal thoughts and feelings
   b. facts
   c. both **a** and **b**

   _____

B. Lindamichellebaron uses facts and feelings to express her viewpoint. Explain her viewpoint in your own words. Then list two of her facts and two of her feelings that helped you find that viewpoint.

_____

_____

_____

_____

_____

_____

_____

Applying Author's Viewpoint

A. Read the following passage, looking for clues that provide facts and for those that show the author's thoughts and feelings. Then follow the directions below.

> *We sang a song that night that had its origins as a spiritual, but the civil rights movement had adopted it [and] sang it with a more rapid tempo. The simple words, I think, really captured the feeling that was in me and—I hoped—the others who were there.*
>
> from *Selma, Lord, Selma: Girlhood Memories of the Civil Rights Days* by Rachel West Nelson

1. List two facts and two feelings presented in the passage.

_____

_____

_____

2. What is the author's viewpoint in this essay?

_____

_____

_____

3. How might the essay be different if the writer had not included her thoughts and feelings?

_____

_____

_____

B. Write a few sentences telling about a book or story you have enjoyed. Provide facts and your own thoughts and feelings about the book.

_____

_____

_____

_____

_____

_____

_____

To review

↓

page 86

Context Clues

| *Lesson 10* | Introducing page 78 | Practicing page 79 | Applying page 80 | Reviewing page 88 | Testing page 89 |

Introducing Strategies

As they read, good readers do not stop to look up every word that they do not know. Instead, they try to figure out the meaning of an unfamiliar word from its **context**, or the way the word is used in a sentence. Good readers know that words and ideas surrounding the unknown word often give clues to its meaning. The strategy below shows how to use **context clues** to define an unfamiliar word.

USING CONTEXT CLUES			
Ask Yourself:	**Yes**	**/ No**	**If Yes:**
Can I find a word or words with a meaning similar to the unfamiliar word?	☐	☐	Write the word or words.
Can I find a word or words with a meaning opposite to the unfamiliar word?	☐	☐	Write the word or words.
Can I find words and ideas that give clues to the meaning of the unfamiliar word?	☐	☐	Copy these clues and/or describe them in your own words.
What is the meaning of the word?			

Reading the Essay

Reread "What's in a Name?" on pages 81-83. Circle any unfamiliar words you find and underline their context clues. Then complete the items below.

1. Find the word *glib* in the essay and tell what the word means. What context clue helped you define it?

_____

_____

2. Find the word *radicals* in the essay and give two clues that helped you define it.

_____

_____

Practicing Context Clues

A. Read the passages below. Then circle the letters of all of the items that give context clues to the meaning of the word in italic type. On the lines that follow, explain your choices.

1. "You dressed only in African *attire* or jeans. You would not be caught speaking standard English in public. Your hair would not be worn straight, even if it naturally was that way."

   a. "dressed"
   b. "jeans"
   c. "standard English"
   d. "hair"

   _____

   _____

2. "We of African descent should never forget what our people have survived. At the same time, we must remind the world of our total history. Our heritage goes beyond slavery, and all of it is woven into the *fabric* of America. Pull out a thread, and the cloth will completely unravel."

   a. "of African descent"
   b. "woven"
   c. "pull out a thread"
   d. "cloth will completely unravel"

   _____

   _____

B. Look in a dictionary to find a word you do not know. After you read the definition, write two sentences using the word. Provide context clues to its meaning.

   _____

   _____

   _____

   _____

   _____

   _____

   _____

   _____

   _____

Applying Context Clues

A. Read the following passage about the rice Japanese people eat. Then answer the questions below it.

The white rice used by most Japanese has lost many of its minerals. In polishing the rice, the inner skin and the heart or germ of the rice are removed, leaving only the kernel. This removes much of the food value. In recent years, the Japanese have learned to balance their diet with other foods.
from *Japan: Land and People by Lorraine D. Peterson*

1. Find the word *polishing* in the passage. On the lines below, write the context clues that helped you understand its meaning. Then write the meaning of *polishing*.

_____

_____

_____

2. What is the definition of the phrase *food value*? What context clues helped you find the meaning of this phrase?

_____

_____

_____

3. Based on the context clues in the passage, write what you learned about rice.

_____

_____

_____

B. What is your favorite dinner? Describe it on the lines below. Are there any foods that might be unfamiliar to your readers? Use context clues to help readers understand how these foods look, taste, and smell.

_____

_____

_____

_____

_____

To review
↓
page 88

Lindamichellebaron (1950-   ) was born in New York City. While attending junior high school in Queens, she took English classes from the African American poet James Clifton Morris. He inspired her to become a poet and an educator. She is currently working on her Ph.D. at Columbia University. She enjoys presenting her poems to children of all ages and has created a name for this job: "edutainer."

What's in a Name?

by Lindamichellebaron

I often hear the same questions. "Why do you write your name all together? Why write three names with no spaces in between and only one capital letter?" Sometimes I answer, "I write my name all together because I *am* together." That's the flip, glib, smooth, "I'm hip" answer. But it's not the true answer.

To understand why I write my name this way, you have to take a trip through time with me. The journey connects my heritage to my decision to write my name as I do. It starts in 1962, when I was 12 years old.

I was in junior high in Queens, New York. Blackness and African-ness were not welcome in that world. We were Negroes then. Sometimes we called ourselves Colored. We did not call each other "black" without picking a fight. You called someone "black" as an insult. You might start with, "You're so black . . ." or "Your mama's so black . . ." or you might just call a person "black and ugly." The world was taught to look at black and the source of blackness—Africa—as bad, ugly, less than.

Many classroom films, textbooks, and magazines helped convince us that Africa held no history worth noting. The movie *Tarzan, King of the Jungle* did not come to our rescue. Tarzan and Jane were the saviors of "primitive" Africans. Even Cheetah, the pet monkey, seemed to have more sense than the African natives—and the natives looked like *us*. We laughed through our discomfort.

As a result, if a person's name even rhymed with an African country, we teased him or her. One of my friends suffered greatly from a constant rhyme: "Mildred Mungo from the Congo."

Then I became confused. The year we learned that Egypt was considered the center of civilization, I located it on the map. Egypt was in Africa. The map had to be

The notes in the margin show how one good reader recognized the author's viewpoint in this essay. He or she considered the facts chosen as well as the thoughts and feelings the author presented.

◀ I bet the essay will tell us why she does write her name this way. This might be her viewpoint.

◀ Here's another fact. She's telling where she went to school and what school was like then.

◀ Here are some facts about what things were like for African Americans in 1962.

◀ Information the young people have been given leads them to act this way. I wonder why she's chosen this fact.

◀ There are facts here, but we also get her personal feelings. She wasn't proud of her heritage. I bet she feels differently now.

wrong. I had been taught it was in the Middle East. I looked and looked for the body of water that separated the two areas. There was no separation.

The late 1960s and early 1970s held many other surprises. New classes called Black Studies introduced us to a new concept, *black and beautiful*. We found out that Ghana, Mali, and Songhai had been empires in West Africa before the year 1000. We were amazed to learn that at the time Africans were being enslaved, Timbuktu was the site of the world-class University of Sankore. Large areas of Africa had cultural and economic institutions much older than those in Europe.

And so we came to discover Africa's history. It had always been there. We just hadn't known about it. We sang along with James Brown, "Say it loud, I'm black and I'm proud." We wore our hair naturally and called it Afro. We wore African-styled clothing. Many of us chose to change our names to reflect a connection to the Motherland, Africa. While others shed their "slave names," I kept my name, Linda Michelle Baron. I saw it as part of my own history.

We also learned about the thriving culture of African Americans. I fell in love with the poets of the 1940s. They spoke of their experiences as Americans who were black. I liked their rhythms, their styles, and their themes. Their images of black as something good, desirable, and wonderful shone through. I was among the young, unknown poets who followed their lead. Even as I followed, however, I knew that I had to let my own heart, mind, and style lead me to my creative self.

As part of this new awareness, young black radicals started to define what it meant to be black. According to their guidelines, if you owned a house, you were not truly black. The "right on" black person had to live in the ghetto. You did not, under any circumstances, play golf or tennis. You dressed only in African attire or jeans. You would not be caught speaking standard English in public. Your hair should not be worn straight, even if it naturally was that way.

I did not want to be defined in these ways. An excerpt from a poem I wrote during that period shows my thoughts:

> I wish I knew how it would feel to be black,
> Not act *like* or be *like*,
> Just be black.
> Some puppet show no go.
> Black, with no strings attached.
> Black, without having to prove black.
> Sky don't act blue.
> Oranges don't have to define the
> behavioral patterns of orange.

I also refused to follow the lead of those who changed their names. I understood why they did it, but I didn't choose to do so. My name reflected my relationship with my mother and my father. I could not shed that connection. Yes, I was proud to be of African descent. No, I was not going to change a name that had its own history in America.

We of African descent should never forget what our people have survived. At the same time, we must remind the world of our total history. Our heritage goes beyond slavery, and all of it is woven into the fabric of America. Pull out a thread, and the cloth will completely unravel.

This is what I want my name to suggest. I want people to ask, "What is she, African or something?" My answer is, "Yes. And American."

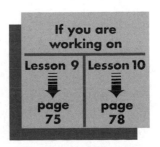

If you are
working on

Lesson 9	Lesson 10
↓	↓
page 75	page 78

Darryl Wilson is a member of the Pitt River Nation. He currently lives in Tucson, where he writes and teaches Native American Studies at the University of Arizona. In the following essay, Wilson describes, from a Native American point of view, what happened in one battle between Native Americans and the U.S. Army.

Little Bighorn: A Native American Perspective

by Darryl Babe Wilson

As you read, write your own ideas in the margins about the author's viewpoint. Think about the facts the writer includes, as well as the thoughts and feelings he expresses.

The Battle of Little Bighorn had its roots during the 1870s, when white miners invaded *Paha Sapa*, the sacred Black Hills of the Sioux Nation. By coming on this land in search of gold, the miners were violating a treaty between the Sioux and the U.S. government. The treaty, agreed to in 1868, said that no white people would be allowed to settle upon or pass through any part of the *Paha Sapa* without the permission of the Native Americans.

To protest the treaty violations, two Sioux chiefs, Red Cloud and Spotted Tail, traveled to Washington, D.C. The government decided that it was time to quiet the criticism of the Native Americans, so they decided to take possession of all the land in and around *Paha Sapa*.

What was done was this. On December 3, 1875, Commissioner of Indian Affairs Edward P. Smith ordered government agents in charge of the Sioux and Cheyenne to tell all Native Americans that they must report their whereabouts by the end of January. Once the government knew where all the Native Americans were living, they could order them to a reservation. Military force would be used if the Native Americans did not follow orders.

Because Native Americans were busy with their daily tasks of hunting, fishing, and gathering food, they had little time to respond. They had other duties as well, of course, including caring for their children and their elderly. They could not leave their homes to make a long journey—especially a journey that made no sense. Remember that they were living on land that was legally theirs and they were not breaking the treaty.

Many of the Sioux did not register with their agents, so the government labeled them "hostile." By February 1876, the War Department had authorized the army to begin moving against these Native Americans.

Leading the Sioux were Chiefs Sitting Bull, Crazy Horse, and Gall. They knew that they were going to be attacked. Sitting Bull went alone into the Black Hills seeking a dream that would show him how to defend his people's homeland. That dream was given to him. He was prepared to win the battle at Greasy Grass Meadow on the Little Bighorn River before a single shot was fired.

The United States officer in charge was General Philip Sheridan. However, it was Lieutenant Colonel George Armstrong Custer, known to the Sioux as *Pahuska* ("Long Hair, Yellow Hair"), who would lead the actual attack that has become known as the Battle of Little Bighorn. Custer wanted the glory that a victory would give him, so he went against orders and launched his attack on June 25, 1876.

As the Seventh Cavalry, led by Custer, poured down the hillside toward the Greasy Grass Meadow, they were met by Sioux on three sides. The Sioux fought according to Sitting Bull's dream. The battle was quickly over, with the Sioux victorious. But there were many battles to come.

Among the Sioux, the Battle of Little Bighorn is viewed as just another conflict. In all their battles, the Sioux were fighting for their land and their lives. They knew that General Sherman, the top-ranking U.S. Army officer, had told his troops that they must act with revenge to exterminate men, women, and children.

The United States, however, has always viewed the Battle of Little Bighorn as extremely important. This is because the Sioux wiped out the U.S. Army forces involved. Therefore, the army had to glorify the battle and make their follow-up actions seem justified. In reporting Custer's death, the army even stated that he was a general, rather than a lieutenant colonel.

Paha Sapa was eventually taken from the Sioux, and many lives were lost. Some of the more important battles to Native Americans were those in which many of their people were killed.

The treaties remain. However, they are meaningless as long as people other than the Sioux live on the sacred lands.

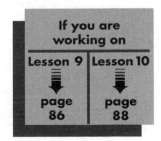

If you are working on

Lesson 9	Lesson 10
⬇	⬇
page 86	page 88

Reviewing Author's Viewpoint

**A. Read "Little Bighorn: A Native American Perspective"
on pages 84-85. As you read, take notes about the facts,
thoughts, and feelings the author presents. Use this
information to explore the author's viewpoint on the
chart below.**

Facts

Thoughts and Feelings

AUTHOR'S VIEWPOINT

**B. Use the information you gathered in Section A and
write a paragraph explaining the author's viewpoint in
this essay. Be sure to mention the facts and feelings you
found and how they helped you understand the essay.**

_____

_____

_____

_____

_____

_____

_____

_____

_____

Testing Author's Viewpoint

A. Read the following statements from the essay. Check whether the statement is a fact or a thought or feeling. On the line that follows, explain your answer.

1. "The Battle of Little Bighorn had its roots during the 1870s, when white miners invaded *Paha Sapa*."
   [ ] fact   [ ] thought or feeling

   _____

2. "To protest the treaty violations, two Sioux chiefs, Red Cloud and Spotted Tail, traveled to Washington, D.C."
   [ ] fact   [ ] thought or feeling

   _____

3. "The U.S. Army had to glorify the Battle of Little Bighorn and make their follow-up actions seem justified."
   [ ] fact   [ ] thought or feeling

   _____

4. "Some of the more important battles to Native Americans were those in which many of their people were killed."
   [ ] fact   [ ] thought or feeling

   _____

5. "The treaties remain. However, they are meaningless as long as people other than the Sioux live on sacred lands."
   [ ] fact   [ ] thought or feeling

   _____

B. Think of a subject about which you feel strongly. It could be something that is happening in your school or in your community. Write a paragraph in which you express your viewpoint and support it with facts and feelings.

_____

_____

_____

_____

_____

_____

_____

To begin
Lesson 10
⬇
page
78

Reviewing Context Clues

A. Reread "Little Bighorn: A Native American Perspective" on pages 84-85. As you read, circle unfamiliar words and underline context clues to their meaning. Choose one of these words to complete the chart below.

USING CONTEXT CLUES

Ask Yourself:	Yes / No	If Yes:
Can I find a word or words with a meaning similar to the unfamiliar word?	☐ ☐	Write the word or words. _____
Can I find a word or words with a meaning opposite to the unfamiliar word?	☐ ☐	Write the word or words. _____
Can I find words and ideas that give clues to the meaning of the unfamiliar word?	☐ ☐	Copy these clues and/or describe them in your own words. _____ _____

Meaning of the Word _____

B. Use the words *violations, whereabouts, launched, revenge,* and *register* in sentences of your own. Make sure your sentences contain context clues that would help a reader figure out each word's meaning.

_____

_____

_____

_____

_____

_____

_____

_____

Testing Context Clues

A. Read the passage below. Then read it a second time and write the word that best fills each blank. Use context clues to make your selections.

It all started when I let Eddie play in the living room. He's only six, and cute as they come. But he does have his down side, which is a bad temper. When he throws a

_____, I find myself giving in even though I know I
(1)

shouldn't. This happens partly because I like the kid, and

partly—I must _____, or admit, that I like peace
(2)

and quiet. Eddie has this toy robot, a scary, nasty-faced,

_____ little thing, all made of very hard plastic in
(3)

shades of sickly green and puce, which is a sort of ugly bright

pink. It's wearing a _____ costume, something out
(4)

of the twenty-first century, and nasty little shoes with cleats

on the bottom, like _____ wear. Eddie calls this
(5)

_____ and totally un-educational toy *Joe*. To make
(6)

Eddie stop _____, I told him it was OK to play with
(7)

Joe in the living room. And what's the first thing Eddie did?

He took Joe ice skating on the oak coffee table. Pulling the toy

robot across the surface of the table marred, or

_____, the wood in a number of places.
(8)

1. party
   tantrum
   dish

2. say
   confess
   shout out

3. evil-looking
   sweet
   gigantic

4. green
   silly
   futuristic

5. little boys
   tap dancers
   football
      players

6. nasty
   pretty
   charming

7. laughing
   crying and
      screaming
   eating

8. polished
   scratched
   burned

B. Choose one of the words you selected in Section A. What context clues helped you figure out its meaning? Write the word in a new sentence, giving your own context clues to its meaning.

_____

_____

_____

Unit SIX

BECOMING AN ACTIVE READER

Reading an **autobiography** is like getting an inside look into someone's life. Good readers listen carefully to what the writer says about what has happened in his or her life. They also consider that they are only hearing one person's views. Reading an autobiography is like meeting a new friend.

Using Skills and Strategies

One way writers help you understand an autobiography is by describing a series of **causes** and **effects**. You may ask: What happened first? What was its effect? Did that effect cause something else to happen? In this way, you learn why writers have acted in particular ways.

Asking questions about **cultural context** will help you become involved in an autobiography. You may ask: What do I learn about the author's culture from the introductory notes? What are the customs and values of the people in the story? How does what I'm reading compare to my own life?

In this unit, identifying **causes and effects** and recognizing **cultural context** will help you read more actively.

The Autobiography: The Writer's Voice

Autobiographers often tell about their childhood and their family. In this way, they give readers a snapshot of what it is like to live in their culture. Good readers consider these details and compare them to their own experiences. They then add what they have learned to what they already know to gain a better understanding of the subject, and of his or her culture.

Responding to Autobiographies

As good readers respond to an autobiography, they compare their own attitudes and experiences with those of the writer. Jot down your responses in the side margins as you read "Stowaway" and "An African's Adventures in America." These notes will help you remember your thoughts as you discuss the selections with your classmates.

Cause and Effect

| Lesson 11 | Introducing page 91 | Practicing page 92 | Applying page 93 | Reviewing page 103 | Testing page 104 |

Introducing Strategies

A **cause** is an action that brings about a result. This result is called the **effect**. A good reader looks for clues, such as signal words like *because* and *therefore*, to find cause-and-effect relationships. For example, in the sentence *Marta became ill because she worked too hard* the word *because* helps identify the cause of Marta's illness. Her illness then might cause other effects, such as missing school or being unable to go to a dance.

The cause-and-effect chain below shows how one action can influence many other events.

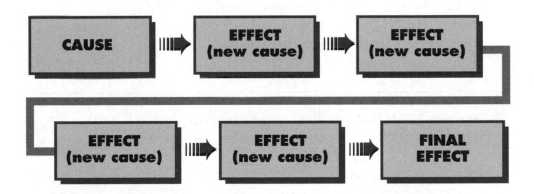

Reading the Essay

Read "Stowaway" by Armando Socarras Ramírez on pages 97-100 and the sidenotes on pages 97-98. The sidenotes show the cause-and-effect relationships one reader found. Use these notes to answer the questions below.

1. List two cause-and-effect relationships the reader found.

_____

_____

2. Change one cause or effect that you listed in #1 above. How would this change affect the rest of the essay?

_____

_____

Practicing Cause and Effect

A. Complete each statement below by choosing the cause that explains each effect. Then, on the line that follows each one, explain your choice.

1. As a stowaway, Armando did not know what happened to Jorge because
   a. Armando passed out.
   b. both teenagers would not fit in the same wheel well.
   c. the sound of the jet engines prevented them from talking to each other.
   d. Jorge jumped from the wheel well and ran into the tall grass to avoid being caught by the police.

   _____

2. Armando left Cuba as a stowaway because
   a. he wanted to have an adventure.
   b. he wanted freedom.
   c. he didn't want to pay the airfare.
   d. he was in love.

   _____

3. Armando almost died as a stowaway in a wheel well because
   a. he was squashed by the wheels.
   b. he fell out of the wheel well.
   c. he was arrested by Cuban police.
   d. his body temperature dropped dangerously.

   _____

B. How did escaping from Cuba affect Jorge's life?

   _____

   _____

   _____

   _____

   _____

   _____

   _____

   _____

Applying Cause and Effect

A. Read the paragraphs below. Look for context clues that answer the questions *What happened?* and *Why did it happen?* Then answer the questions that follow.

> *"It's hard to make friends here," Ling said. "Back home, my best friend and I used to call each other every day after school. Michelle, do people here share phone numbers?"*
>
> *I tried not to gasp. My secret was sure to get out. For two weeks my family had been without a phone. What if everyone found out we were too poor to pay our phone bill? I quickly changed the subject.*
>
> *The next day Ling walked home with someone new.*

1. Why does Ling want to share phone numbers with Michelle?

_____

_____

2. What effect does Ling's question have on Michelle? Explain your answer.

_____

_____

3. What do you think caused Ling to walk home with someone else the next day?

_____

_____

B. Write a paragraph explaining what Michelle might have done to cause Ling to remain her friend.

_____

_____

_____

_____

_____

_____

_____

_____

To review

↓

page
103

Cultural Context

| **Lesson 12** | Introducing page 94 | Practicing page 95 | Applying page 96 | Reviewing page 105 | Testing page 106 |

Introducing Strategies

Good readers begin looking for **cultural context** by reading the introductory notes about an author. Readers continue their search by gathering details about the customs, values, and language of the culture shown in the essay. They then compare this information with what they know about their own culture. When they learn about cultural context, readers gain a greater understanding of the writer, the culture shown in the essay, and themselves.

The diagram below shows how readers can combine these details to learn about culture.

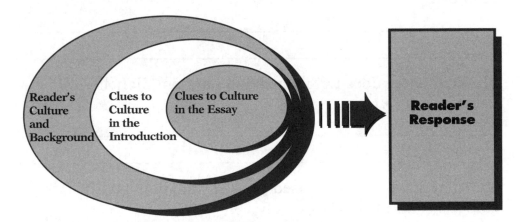

Reader's Culture and Background — Clues to Culture in the Introduction — Clues to Culture in the Essay → Reader's Response

Reading the Essay

Reread "Stowaway" on pages 97-100. As you read, underline the information you find about Cuban culture. Use these notes to answer the questions below.

1. List at least three details from the essay that describe Cuba as Armando sees it.

_____

_____

_____

2. What does Armando expect to find in the United States?

_____

_____

Practicing Cultural Context

A. Circle the letter of the choice that best completes each statement below. Then, on the line that follows, explain your choice.

1. One of the things Armando enjoyed about his life in Cuba was
   a. dancing with María.
   b. playing baseball.
   c. going to the theater.
   d. going to family festivals.

_____

2. Before he went away to welding school, Armando
   a. lived in a one-room house.
   b. had to share scarce food.
   c. lived with 10 other people.
   d. all of the above

_____

3. Armando knew his uncle would
   a. want Armando to stay in Cuba.
   b. buy Armando a plane ticket to the United States.
   c. give Armando a home in the United States.
   d. send Armando to art school.

_____

B. How do you think this essay might be different if it were written by someone who wanted to escape from a different country?

_____

_____

_____

_____

_____

_____

_____

_____

Applying Cultural Context

A. Read the following passage about a young man who leaves the city for a teaching job in the countryside of Nicaragua. Then answer the questions that follow it.

> *I never worked in my house [in Managua]. But in the country I learned how to plant corn and beans. I learned how to pick coffee beans and how to milk cows. And to eat foods that were very different.*
>
> *But the first thing you learn is how to carry a stick and a machete when you're out walking. One day I was almost bitten by a poisonous snake. The twelve-year-old killed the snake with his machete. That snake could have killed me or left me crazy. The nearest doctor was four hours away.*
> *told by Evenor Ortega for Inside Nicaragua*

1. Identify three details that tell about working in the countryside of Nicaragua.

_____

_____

_____

2. Identify a detail that tells about nature in the Nicaraguan countryside.

_____

B. How does the culture in this passage differ from another culture you know about? Write a paragraph on the lines below to explain. Be sure to give examples.

_____

_____

_____

_____

_____

_____

_____

_____

_____

To review
⬇
page
105

This essay tells the story of Armando Socarras Ramírez (1952-   ). His homeland is Cuba, a Communist country under the dictatorship of Fidel Castro. Few people are allowed to leave Cuba legally, though many are desperate for a better life. In 1970 Armando took a risk to escape.

Stowaway

by Armando Socarras Ramírez

The notes in the margin show how one reader recognized cause-and-effect relationships in the essay.

The jet engines of the Iberia Airlines DC-8 thundered in ear-splitting crescendo as the big plane taxied toward where we huddled in the tall grass just off the end of the runway at Havana's José Martí Airport. For months, my friend Jorge Pérez Blanco and I had been planning to stow away in a wheel well on this flight, No. 904— Iberia's once-weekly, nonstop run from Havana to Madrid. Now, in the late afternoon of June 3, 1970, our moment had come.

We realized that we were pretty young to be taking such a big gamble; I was seventeen, Jorge sixteen. But we were both determined to escape from Cuba, and our plans had been carefully made. We knew that departing airliners taxied to the end of the 11,500-foot runway, stopped momentarily after turning around, then roared at full throttle down the runway to take off. We wore rubber-soled shoes to aid us in crawling up the wheels and carried ropes to secure ourselves inside the wheel well. We had also stuffed cotton in our ears as protection against the shriek of the four jet engines. Now we lay sweating with fear as the massive craft swung into its about-face, the jet blast flattening the grass all around us. "Let's run!" I shouted to Jorge.

◀ Wanting to escape from Cuba caused Armando and Jorge to stow away in the plane.

We dashed onto the runway and sprinted toward the left-hand wheels of the momentarily stationary plane. As Jorge began to scramble up the 42-inch-high tires, I saw there was not room for us both in the single well. "I'll try the other side!" I shouted. Quickly I climbed onto the right wheels, grabbed a strut, and, twisting and wriggling, pulled myself into the semi-dark well. The plane began rolling immediately, and I grabbed some machinery to keep from falling out. The roar of the engines nearly deafened me.

◀ Armando won't be able to see or talk to Jorge during the flight. This is the effect of the wheel well's being too small for two people.

As we became airborne, the huge double wheels, scorching hot from takeoff, began folding into the compartment. I tried to flatten myself against the overhead as they came closer and closer; then, in desperation, I pushed at them with my feet. But they pressed powerfully upward, squeezing me terrifyingly against the roof of the well. Just when I felt that I would be crushed, the wheels locked in place and the bay doors beneath them closed, plunging me into darkness. So there I was, my five-foot-four-inch 140-pound frame literally wedged in amid a spaghettilike maze of conduits and machinery. I could not move enough to tie myself to anything, so I stuck my rope behind a pipe.

Then, before I had time to catch my breath, the bay doors suddenly dropped open again and the wheels stretched out into their landing position. I held on for dear life, swinging over the abyss, wondering if I had been spotted, if even now the plane was turning back to hand me over to Castro's police.

By the time the wheels began retracting again, I had seen a bit of extra space among all the machinery where I could safely squeeze. Now I knew there was room for me, even though I could scarcely breathe. After a few minutes, I touched one of the tires and found that it had cooled off. I swallowed some aspirin tablets against the head-splitting noise and began to wish that I had worn something warmer than my light sport shirt and green fatigues. . . .

Shivering uncontrollably from the bitter cold, I wondered if Jorge had made it into the other wheel well and began thinking about what had brought me to this desperate situation. I thought about my parents and my girl, María Esther, and wondered what they would think when they learned what I had done.

My father is a plumber, and I have four brothers and a sister. We are poor, like most Cubans. Our house in Havana has just one large room; eleven people live in it—or did. Food was scarce and strictly rationed. About the only fun I had was playing baseball and walking with María Esther along the seawall. When I turned sixteen, the government shipped me off to vocational school in Betancourt, a sugarcane village in Matanzas Province. There I was supposed to learn welding, but classes were often interrupted to send us off to plant cane.

Young as I was, I was tired of living in a state that controlled everyone's life. I dreamed of freedom. I wanted to become an artist and live in the United States, where I had an uncle. I knew that thousands of Cubans had got to America and done well there. As the time approached when I would be drafted, I thought more and more of

trying to get away. But how? I knew that two planeloads of people are allowed to leave Havana for Miami each day, but there is a waiting list of eight hundred thousand for these flights. Also, if you sign up to leave, the government looks on you as a *gusano*—a worm—and life becomes even less bearable.

My hopes seemed futile. Then I met Jorge at a Havana baseball game. After the game we got to talking. I found out that Jorge, like myself, was disillusioned with Cuba. "The system takes away your freedom—forever," he complained.

Jorge told me about the weekly flight to Madrid. Twice we went to the airport to reconnoiter. Once a DC-8 took off and flew directly over us; the wheels were still down, and we could see into the well compartments. "There's enough room in there for me," I remember saying.

These were my thoughts as I lay in the freezing darkness more than five miles above the Atlantic Ocean. By now we had been in the air about an hour, and I was getting light-headed from the lack of oxygen. Was it really only a few hours earlier that I had bicycled through the rain with Jorge and hidden in the grass? Was Jorge safe? My parents? María Esther? I drifted into unconsciousness. . . .

The first thing I remember after losing consciousness was hitting the ground at the Madrid airport. Then I blacked out again and woke up later at the Gran Hospital de la Beneficencia in downtown Madrid, more dead than alive. When they took my temperature, it was so low that it did not even register on the thermometer. "Am I in Spain?" was my first question. And then, "Where's Jorge?" (Jorge is believed to have been knocked down by the jet blast while trying to climb into the other wheel well, and to be in prison in Cuba.)

Doctors said later that my condition was comparable to that of a patient undergoing "deep freeze" surgery—a delicate process performed under carefully controlled conditions. Dr. José María Pajares, who cared for me, called my survival a "medical miracle," and, in truth, I feel lucky to be alive.

A few days after my escape, I was up and around the hospital, playing cards with my police guard and reading stacks of letters from all over the world. I especially liked one from a girl in California. "You are a hero," she wrote, "but not very wise." My uncle, Elo Fernández, who lives in New Jersey, telephoned and invited me to come to the United States to live with him. The International Rescue Committee arranged my passage and has continued to help me.

I am fine now. I live with my uncle and go to school to learn English. I still hope to study to be an artist. I want to be a good citizen and contribute something to this country, for I love it here. You can smell freedom in the air.

I often think of my friend Jorge. We both knew the risk we were taking, and that we might be killed in our attempt to escape Cuba. But it seemed worth the chance. Even knowing the risks, I would try to escape again if I had to.

If you are working on

Lesson 11	Lesson 12
⬇	⬇
page 91	page 94

The following is an excerpt from an essay written by Babs Fafunwa, who came to the United States from Nigeria to attend college. In 1948, when he arrived, he found that some people had strange ideas about Africans, and that some aspects of life in America were not what he expected.

An African's Adventures in America

by Babs Fafunwa

As you read, make notes about how recognizing causes and effects helps you understand Fafunwa's adventures.

Since my arrival in this country, I have met over fifty African students during my vacations. In exchanging views with them I found that most of our impressions after arriving on American soil are almost identical. Everything about him is new, the student finds out.

He is mobbed by a group of inquiring reporters who ask: What is your name? Where do you come from? What is your impression about America? How many wives has your father? Are you married? Is it true that you buy women in Africa? Are you a prince? Is your father a king or a gold miner?

The shooting of flash bulbs adds to the confusion. This barrage is an indication of what the student is to experience as he moves from one part of the United States to another.

One of my most exciting experiences happened when I arrived in New York City. On that day it had one of its greatest snowfalls, and what's more I had never seen snow in my life. That day, my heavy overcoat was no solution to my dilemma. As I stepped out of the airplane I was baptized with the unusually biting cold. I was shaken to the bones and all my limbs were trembling. The woman in me subdued the man and my eyes were shedding tears like an Arabian gum tree. That night I slept in my overcoat, suit and all. The temperature was 19° F and the lowest temperature I have ever seen in Nigeria is 60°.

Till I landed in New York I had never met an American Negro. My impression was that since the Negro has been living there for the past three hundred years or more he ought to have intermarried with the whites so that his color should be at least lighter than my own. (By the way, I am ebony black and I'd like to be twice as dark.) But when I landed I saw a Negro darker than myself. I thought he was an African who came a little earlier than I did. I rushed to him with all the happiness and the joy of finding a kinsman in this great metropolis. I said, "Hello, dear, when did you come?" He looked at me with cold surprise. I later found that he must have been here three hundred years, for his speech is as entirely strange to me as mine to him. . . .

The student finds that democracy works fairly well in the North and otherwise in the South. He finds in the North that competition is tough, but in the South segregation and discrimination stare him in the face. I remember one day when the African students at Bethune-Cookman College in Florida were on their way back to school after giving an African program at a church. We stopped at a filling station for some refreshments.

A policeman entered and said, "Where are you 'niggers' from?"

We quickly responded that we were not niggers but African students.

"I say you are niggers," he shouted.

"No, 'officer of peace,' we are not."

"I say you are niggers," he affirmed, and to make it more positive he rested his hand on his gun. Like cowards we had to admit that we were niggers—at least by keeping silent!

We have been turned out of restaurants in the South several times despite our appeal to the people in charge that we are strangers and that such action is un-American since it is bad public relations for America, the arena of democracy. It is very encouraging, however, to find that once in a while we meet people in the South who give us very good breaks, help and assistance. Once a white fellow gave me a ride, and as I entered I sat at the back, for you are not supposed to sit with a white. He said, "Come to the front—I am no chauffeur." I was amused indeed.

The denial of the ballot box to Negroes in some parts of the South makes the average African student become a little disillusioned about American democracy. He believed before coming to America that this country is an arsenal of democracy, but to his dismay he finds that America is just learning like Africa to be democratic. Who knows, the whole world might soon copy Africa as regards true democracy.

If you are working on

Lesson 11 | Lesson 12

page 103 | page 105

Reviewing Cause and Effect

A. Read "An African's Adventures in America" on pages 101-102. Then use the chart below to show how understanding causes and effects helps you to follow Fafunwa's essay.

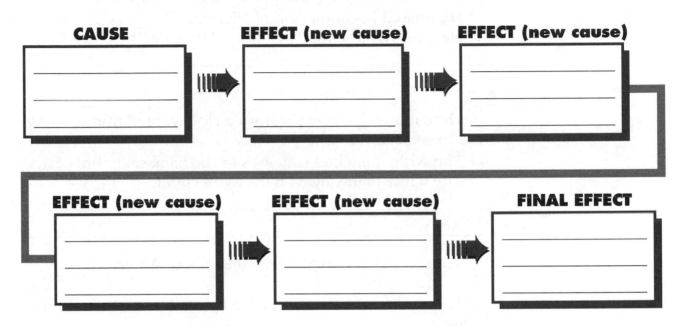

B. In the late 1940s, Babs Fafunwa felt that the average African student coming to the United States might discover that the country was still learning to be a true democracy. Explain what caused him to feel this way.

_____

_____

_____

_____

_____

_____

_____

_____

_____

_____

Testing Cause and Effect

A. For each item below, fill in the bubble next to the cause for each action. Then, on the lines provided, explain why you answered as you did.

1. Fafunwa cried the day he arrived in New York City.
   ○ He missed his homeland of Nigeria.
   ○ He was overwhelmed by the cold weather.

_____

_____

2. A white man who gave Fafunwa a ride wanted him to sit in the front seat.
   ○ The white man had suitcases in the back seat of his car.
   ○ The white man viewed Babs as an equal.

_____

_____

3. African students were disillusioned about American democracy.
   ○ Many African Americans were being denied the right to vote.
   ○ People in the United States reject all ideas of class.

_____

_____

B. Imagine you are Fafunwa and write a journal entry in which you explain how one of the things you have seen in the United States has affected you.

_____

_____

_____

_____

_____

_____

_____

_____

_____

To begin Lesson 12 ⬇ page 94

Reviewing Cultural Context

A. Reread the essay "An African's Adventures in America" on pages 101-102. As you read, underline details about U.S. culture as Fafunwa experienced it in the late 1940s. Note how this culture is similar to and different from your own culture. Then use the chart below to record your responses.

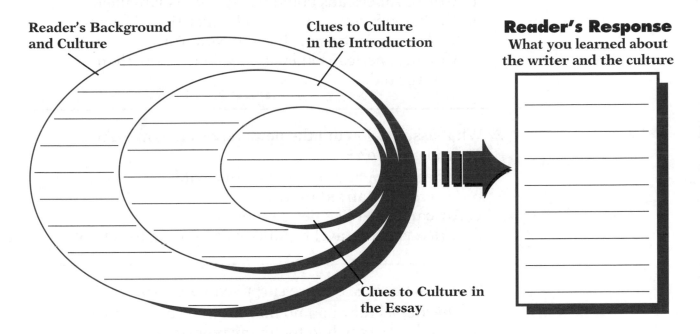

Reader's Background and Culture

Clues to Culture in the Introduction

Clues to Culture in the Essay

Reader's Response
What you learned about the writer and the culture

B. Imagine you have just arrived in your town from another country. Write a brief description of the cultural details you might notice.

_____

_____

_____

_____

_____

_____

_____

_____

_____

_____

Testing Cultural Context

A. Circle the letter of the best answer for each question below. Then, on the line provided, explain why you answered as you did.

1. What was one cultural difference that Fafunwa experienced?

   a. African Americans could not speak his language.
   b. African Americans were much taller than Africans.
   c. No African Americans lived in New York.
   d. African Americans knew more about snow than Africans did.

   _____

2. What assumption did the news reporters make about African culture?

   a. African men have more than one wife.
   b. Africans are afraid to travel.
   c. Africans don't like news reporters.
   d. Africans who travel to America are going to school.

   _____

3. What part of U.S. culture surprised Fafunwa?

   a. This democracy had no interest in foreign students.
   b. This democracy had too many reporters.
   c. This democracy was not yet perfect.
   d. This democracy had a very cold climate.

   _____

B. Give an example from the essay of a detail that reveals something about Fafunwa's African culture. Explain what that detail tells you about the culture.

   _____

   _____

   _____

   _____

   _____

   _____

   _____

   _____

Unit SEVEN

BECOMING AN ACTIVE READER

Reading a **poem** is like looking at art or hearing a musical masterpiece. It can help you feel what the poet feels and see what the poet sees. In this way, you can draw a mental picture that will guide you to the poem's meaning.

Using Skills and Strategies

Asking questions about the **speaker of a poem** will help you understand it. You may ask: Is someone telling me what is happening in this poem? Who is this person? What are the speaker's feelings? Have I had similar feelings? Do I know anyone like this?

One way poets touch their readers' emotions is by creating a **mood** with words. You may ask: What feelings did I have as I read the poem? What feeling did I have when I finished reading? What words make me feel this way?

In this unit, identifying the **speaker of a poem** and the poem's **mood** will help you read poetry more actively.

The Poem: The Writer's Voice

Poems from all cultures help us see that we share many feelings and thoughts with people around the world. You may learn that everyone sometimes feels embarrassed, left out, or proud. You may also learn new ways to see and appreciate the world around you.

Responding to Poetry

Good readers often have strong reactions to poems. They feel as excited, sad, or hopeful as the poet seems to feel. Jot down your feelings and thoughts in the side margins as you read "Poetry Lesson Number One" and "Gaining Yardage." Writing sidenotes will help you think about individual images. Use these notes to help you remember your responses as you discuss the poems with your classmates.

Speaker of a Poem

| *Lesson 13* | Introducing page 108 | Practicing page 109 | Applying page 110 | Reviewing page 117 | Testing page 118 |

Introducing Strategies

To understand poetry, good readers ask themselves if someone is speaking in a poem. The **speaker** is the character who tells what is happening. As you read poetry, ask yourself if someone is talking. If so, think about what this character is like. What words in the poem provide clues about this? The diagram below shows how you can figure out who the speaker is and what he or she is like.

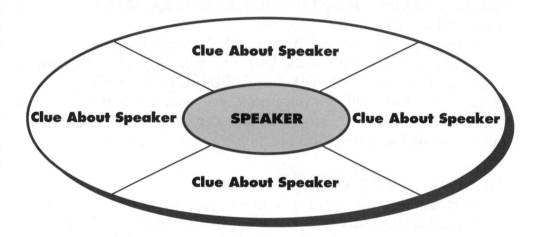

Reading the Poem

Read "Poetry Lesson Number One" on pages 114-115 and the sidenotes on page 114. The sidenotes show how one reader gathered clues about the speaker of the poem. Use these notes to complete the items below.

1. List two clues about the speaker of the poem that the reader found.

_____

_____

2. What clue led the reader to decide that the speaker of the poem is brave?

_____

_____

Practicing Speaker of a Poem

A. The statements below are about "Poetry Lesson Number One." In each pair, only one of the statements is true. Fill in the bubble next to each true statement. Then, on the lines that follow, explain your answer.

1. ○ The speaker in this poem thinks she is "of exceptional beauty."
   ○ The speaker in the poem wants Cleveland and his friends to read her poetry.

   _____

   _____

   _____

2. ○ The speaker is so nervous about the guys reading her poems that she is almost ill.
   ○ The speaker wants to talk about school with Cleveland and the other guys.

   _____

   _____

   _____

3. ○ The speaker leaves the café feeling mean and unhappy.
   ○ On her way home, the speaker is very happy.

   _____

   _____

   _____

B. Who says that the speaker is "as good a writer as a man"? How does the speaker feel about this statement? Explain your thinking.

   _____

   _____

   _____

   _____

   _____

   _____

Applying Speaker of a Poem

A. Read the excerpt below, which is from the poem "Ole Man River" by Marsha Barrett Lippincott. Then complete the items that follow it.

The Mississippi River is an unreasonable place to learn to ski . . .
when I'd fall, waiting there in the channel
to be saved yet again by my father,
trees on the bank whizzed past, and I was in awe.
Take that motorboat to sand bars, spend the day half in
    Arkansas
sing, in Southern, "It's a treat to beat your feet in the
    Mississippi mud."

1. Who is the speaker of this poem? Give a clue from the poem to support your answer.

_____

_____

_____

2. Write a one- or two-sentence description of the speaker. Support your description with lines from the poem.

_____

_____

_____

_____

B. What advice do you think the speaker might give later in the poem? Explain your answer using clues you've found in the poem about the speaker.

_____

_____

_____

_____

_____

_____

To review
↓
page
117

Mood

| Lesson 14 | Introducing page 111 | Practicing page 112 | Applying page 113 | Reviewing page 119 | Testing page 120 |

Introducing Strategies

Mood is the overall feeling of a work of literature. The mood of a piece of writing can be joyful, sad, quiet, serious, or some combination of emotions. Poets create mood with the subjects they choose and the words they use to tell about these subjects. To figure out the mood of a poem, good readers first look at their own response when they have finished reading. Then they go back and examine the words and phrases that made them feel this way. Finally, they state in their own words the mood of the poem. The diagram below shows how this works.

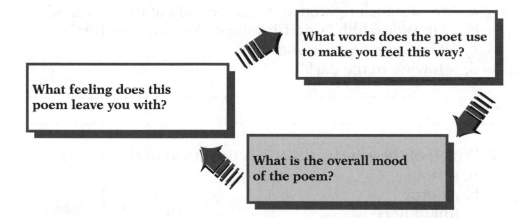

What feeling does this poem leave you with?

What words does the poet use to make you feel this way?

What is the overall mood of the poem?

Reading the Poem

Now reread "Poetry Lesson Number One" on pages 114–115. As you read, underline any words that help you understand the poem's mood. Then complete the items below.

1. Describe what you were thinking when you finished reading the poem.

_____

_____

2. What is the mood, or overall atmosphere, of the poem?

_____

_____

Practicing Mood

A. The statements below are about "Poetry Lesson Number One." Circle the best answer to each question. Then, on the lines that follow, explain your choice.

1. Which of the following groups of words gives an idea of how badly the girl wants to share her poetry?
   a. "No women were allowed at that table"
   b. "starved for approval"
   c. "took it and read it out loud"
   d. "'You are a writer, young lady.'"

   _____

   _____

2. Which group of words from the poem does *not* convey its overall mood?
   a. "my stomach tightened twice for each of my 19 years"
   b. "'Oh yeeeaahhh,' said Cleveland. 'You are a writer'"
   c. "carrying his words with me"
   d. "glowing in the dark"

   _____

   _____

3. Which of these items describes the mood of the poem?
   a. serious
   b. gloomy
   c. full of hope
   d. uncertain

   _____

   _____

B. How do you think the poem would be different if the mood were changed? Explain your answer.

   _____

   _____

   _____

   _____

   _____

   _____

Applying Mood

A. Read the poem below, "Future," by Barbara Field, then complete the items that follow.

I saw the tracks lined with gold and silver.
The coal from Appalachia, the oil from Pennsylvania
heading to the railway depot
in the red light of evening.

Freight trains, great trains
I couldn't wait for change, big
industry, certain livelihood,
work.

1. Describe what you were thinking when you finished reading this poem.

_____

_____

2. List words or phrases from the poem that helped make you feel this way.

_____

_____

_____

3. Describe the mood of this poem.

_____

_____

_____

B. How does understanding a poem's mood help you understand the meaning of a poem?

_____

_____

_____

_____

_____

To review

page
119

Wanda Coleman grew up in the Watts neighborhood of Los Angeles. Later, as a young mother struggling to raise a child on her own, she determined to become a writer or "die in the effort." She has since published four books of poetry and fiction and has won an Emmy for a screenplay.

Poetry Lesson Number One

by Wanda Coleman

The notes in the margin show how one reader gathered clues about the speaker in this poem.

Cleveland and them hung out in that Watts café used
   to be
   across the
tracks on a diagonal north of the workshop off 103rd. No
   women were

▶ *Here are some clues about where the speaker is. Cleveland must be a person the speaker knows.*

allowed at that table unless being schemed upon, or of
   exceptional beauty.
But I was a stubborn little mud hen at the fringe of
   the clique,
   starved

▶ *The speaker is female. She calls herself a "mud hen." I wonder what kind of approval she wants from these guys.*

for approval.

So one day Cleveland and them was sitting at the table.
   Cleve
   and maybe

▶ *The clues in these lines make her seem brave. She walks right up to the table where women are not usually welcome—especially not a "mud hen"—unless the guys are flirting.*

Eric and one other brother. I boldly intruded on their
   exclusivity with
my neat little sheaf of poems.

"And so you write?" and "Let us see one!" And the
   other
   brother took it and
read it out loud and they passed it around the table.
   "Hmmmm" and "Ahhhh."
And I blushed and my stomach tightened twice for each of
   my
   19 years.

"Oh yeeeaahhh," said Cleveland. "You are a writer,
  young
    lady. As good a
writer as a man!"

And I caught the bus home, carrying his words with me,
    clutching my thin
little poems to my heart,

glowing in the dark.

Make your own notes in
the margin about the
speaker of the poem.

If you are
working on

| Lesson 13 | Lesson 14 |
| page 108 | page 111 |

Gaining Yardage

by Leo Dangel

As you read, write your own notes in the margins about the clues you find to the speaker of the poem.

The word *friend* never came up
between Arlo and me—we're farm neighbors
who hang around together, walk beans,
pick rocks, and sit on the bench
at football games, weighing the assets
of the other side's cheerleaders.
Tonight we lead 48 to 6, so the coach
figures sending us both in is safe.
I intercept an underthrown pass
only because I'm playing the wrong position,
and Arlo is right there to block for me
because he's in the wrong place,
so we gallop up the field, in the clear
until their second-string quarterback
meets us at the five-yard line,
determined to make up for his bad throw.
Arlo misses the block, the guy has me
by the leg and jersey, and going down,
I flip the ball back to Arlo, getting up,
who fumbles, and their quarterback
almost recovers, then bobbles the ball
across the goal line, and our coach,
who told even the guys with good hands
never to mess around with laterals,
must feel his head exploding,
when Arlo and I dive on the ball together
in the end zone and dance and slap
each other on the back.
They give Arlo the touchdown, which rightly
should be mine, but I don't mind,
and I suppose we are friends, and will be,
unless my old man or his decides to move
to another part of the country.

If you are
working on

Lesson 13 | Lesson 14

page
117

page
119

| Lesson 13 | Introducing page 108 | Practicing page 109 | Applying page 110 | Reviewing page 117 | Testing page 118 |

Reviewing *Speaker of a Poem*

A. Now read "Gaining Yardage" on page 116. As you read, make notes in the margins about clues you find to the speaker of the poem. Then use the chart below to organize your ideas and describe the speaker.

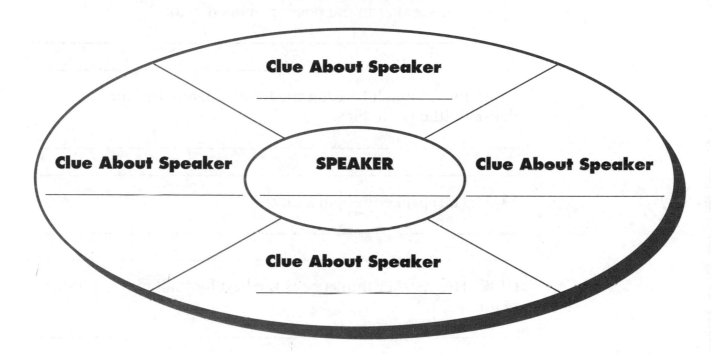

Clue About Speaker

Clue About Speaker   **SPEAKER**   **Clue About Speaker**

Clue About Speaker

B. Would you like to have the speaker for a friend? Explain why you feel as you do.

_____

_____

_____

_____

_____

_____

_____

_____

_____

_____

Testing Speaker of a Poem

A. The statements below are about the poem "Gaining Yardage." Check the box in front of each statement you think can be backed up by clues in the poem. Then, on the lines that follow, explain your answer.

[ ] **1.** The speaker in the poem is named Arlo.

_____

_____

[ ] **2.** Even though he is on the football team, the speaker doesn't often get to play.

_____

_____

[ ] **3.** The speaker lives in a city.

_____

_____

[ ] **4.** The speaker thinks he is the best football player on the team.

_____

_____

[ ] **5.** The speaker is not very emotional, but he still has strong feelings of friendship for his buddy.

_____

_____

B. Choose three words that describe the speaker of this poem. Use clues to write a paragraph describing him.

_____

_____

_____

_____

_____

_____

_____

To begin Lesson 14

page 111

Reviewing Mood

A. Reread "Gaining Yardage" on page 116. What were you thinking when you finished reading the poem? Underline words and phrases that you think help create this response. Use your notes to complete the chart below.

What words make me feel this way?

How do I feel after reading this poem?

What is the mood of the poem?

B. If you were to write a poem about someone who is important in your life, what mood would you want to create? How might you convey this mood?

_____

_____

_____

_____

_____

_____

_____

_____

Testing Mood

A. All the statements below are based on the poem "Gaining Yardage." Circle the number of each statement that you feel can be supported by information in the poem. Explain your response on the lines that follow.

1. This poem leaves the reader feeling impressed at how hard it is to play football well.

_____

_____

2. The mood of this poem is one of great excitement about a football game.

_____

_____

3. The lines "They give Arlo the touchdown, which rightly / should be mine, but I don't mind" suggest that the speaker is angry about the results of the game.

_____

_____

4. The words "hang around together" and "I suppose we are friends, and will be" help create the mood of friendship and happiness in the poem.

_____

_____

B. Suppose you plan to write a poem about a frightening natural occurrence, such as a thunderstorm, a flood, a severe heat wave, or a blizzard. Brainstorm a list of words and phrases that could convey the mood of this poem.

_____

_____

_____

_____

_____

_____

Book Test

PART 1: FICTION

Read the short story below and respond to it by circling key images and writing notes in the margins. Then use the story and your notes to help you answer the questions on the next page.

Moon Child

1 I was born during the full moon in the early 1980s. On my 12th birthday, my Anishinabe grandmother gave me her great-grandmother's pony bead necklace. It was white, blue, and black. My father said, "What a piece of junk," and turned on his football game way too loud. My mother did not look up from the newspaper.

2 In September, my father left for the city and never lived with us again. He said he couldn't stand it anymore. After he left, Mom cried a lot. She called September "the moon of red berries." The next month she called "the moon of falling leaves." By November she hardly cried at all. She did not give the month of November a new name.

3 I was the eldest daughter so I slept by the door. One night in late November, my father came back while my mother and my brothers slept. I saw the whites of his eyes like an owl's as he stood in the doorway and looked in on us. He carried his blanket of red, umber, and yellow. The next morning I didn't know whether to tell my mother or to walk in shadows. I wrote this poem by the canyon:

> The south wind is the color of green
> it brings life energy
> it brings a strong heart
> *wanaki*—now I sing for peace
> *wanaki*—now I breathe for peace
> the wings of my spirit
> will make my voice heard
> along the rocks of the woodland
> and this green, green earth.

4 That evening I talked to my mother and made my voice heard. The next morning the sun rose bright. Mom said she was happy because she dreamed that she, my brothers, and I were laughing. She told me that peace was finally coming to our house. She said I, her moon child, had brought it.

A. Use the selection and your notes to identify the best answer to each question below.

1. The conflict that the moon child faces centers on
   a. whether or not her father will return for her birthday.
   b. whether or not to tell her father the truth.
   c. whether or not her brothers will leave their family.
   d. whether or not to tell her mother that her father came back one night.

2. In paragraph 2, the moon child's father "couldn't stand it anymore." The meaning of this idiom is that
   a. his legs hurt.
   b. he feels his troubles are terrible.
   c. he needs to talk with the family about his troubles.
   d. he is happy with his life.

3. Based on details from the story and what you already know, what conclusion can you draw about the moon child?
   a. She didn't tell her mother that her father came back.
   b. She told her mother that her father came back.
   c. She gave her mother her beaded necklace.
   d. She told her mother that her father would return with the moon.

4. The narrator's mother was happy at the end of the story. This effect is caused by
   a. her dream.
   b. her new blanket.
   c. her husband moving back home.
   d. her daughter's poem.

5. The speaker of the poem that the moon child writes wants
   a. to clean up pollution on the earth.
   b. her father to go away.
   c. to find strength and make her voice heard.
   d. to stay cool in the shadows of the woodland.

6. Which of the following best describes the mood of the moon child's poem?
   a. hopeful
   b. excited
   c. frustrated
   d. angry

B. The narrator has a problem, or conflict, and doesn't know what to tell her mother. Write a solution to the story's problem.

_____

_____

_____

_____

_____

Book Test

PART 2: NONFICTION

Read the article below, which is from a social studies textbook. Respond to it by underlining key words and writing notes in the margins. Then use the article and your notes to answer the questions on the next page.

The Living History of Africa

1 The continent of Africa has a rich and varied history. We've learned about this history from writings and from objects that people have made over the years. The source of most of our information, though, is oral historians.

History in Words

2 Africa's past can be directly traced through its **oral tradition**—spoken history. In the oral tradition, the listener pays close attention to what is said, learns it word-for-word, and thinks about its meanings.

3 The listener then passes on these messages as fables, proverbs, and stories. Oral tradition gives us information about a culture's values, religion, science, entertainment, and history, all in one.

Oral Historians

4 The keepers of this oral tradition are called *the living memory of Africa*. Perhaps the best known of these historians are the **griots**. The most important role a griot can play is to speak for a ruler. According to one source, "the [ruler] speaks softly and the *griot* repeats his words loudly."

5 Griots have been called poets and musical entertainers. But they are far more than that. They collect their culture's oral traditions and pass them on at weddings, feasts, and other occasions.

6 Griots also keep the past alive by recalling the adventures of the region's kings. Thus, the people hear stories about their ancestors and learn about their rich history. Scientific investigations have confirmed much of the history reported by griots.

7 In present-day Africa, few griots still exist. Many have become college history professors. Others have had their oral traditions tape-recorded or written down so that they can continue telling their traditions to the world.

A. Circle the letter before the word or words that best answer each question below.

1. The subtopic **History in Words** contains details about

    a. poets and musical entertainers.
    b. marriage ceremonies in Africa.
    c. Africa's spoken history.
    d. traditionalists called *griots*.

2. Which TWO of the following choices give clues to the meaning of the key word *griot*?

    a. ruler
    b. writer
    c. oral historian
    d. storyteller

3. The main idea of this article is that

    a. griots have tape-recorded their traditions.
    b. the most important source of knowledge about African history is oral historians.
    c. griots entertain people at weddings.
    d. scientific investigations have confirmed much of the history reported by griots.

4. How are today's griots like those of the past?

    a. Both wrote down their stories.
    b. Both performed a weekly ceremony to honor their king.
    c. Both would not let their words be recorded.
    d. Both passed on Africa's history.

5. What is the author's viewpoint?

    a. African history has been lost.
    b. The stories told by the griots provide a rich picture of the past.
    c. Africans can learn more about history by reading than by listening to griots.
    d. Oral traditions should be valued only as entertainment.

6. What context clue helps you define the words *oral tradition* in paragraph 2?

    a. "the listener pays close attention to what is said"
    b. "spoken history"
    c. "word-for-word"
    d. all of the above

B. Use at least three details from the passage to describe how African history has been passed on.

_____

_____

_____

_____

_____

_____

_____

_____

_____